STRATEGIC STUDIES INSTITUTE

I0408730

The Strategic Studies Institute (SSI) is part of the U.S. Army War College and is the strategic-level study agent for issues related to national security and military strategy with emphasis on geostrategic analysis.

The mission of SSI is to use independent analysis to conduct strategic studies that develop policy recommendations on:

- Strategy, planning, and policy for joint and combined employment of military forces;

- Regional strategic appraisals;

- The nature of land warfare;

- Matters affecting the Army's future;

- The concepts, philosophy, and theory of strategy; and,

- Other issues of importance to the leadership of the Army.

Studies produced by civilian and military analysts concern topics having strategic implications for the Army, the Department of Defense, and the larger national security community.

In addition to its studies, SSI publishes special reports on topics of special or immediate interest. These include edited proceedings of conferences and topically oriented roundtables, expanded trip reports, and quick-reaction responses to senior Army leaders.

The Institute provides a valuable analytical capability within the Army to address strategic and other issues in support of Army participation in national security policy formulation.

The United States Army War College

The United States Army War College educates and develops leaders for service at the strategic level while advancing knowledge in the global application of Landpower.

The purpose of the United States Army War College is to produce graduates who are skilled critical thinkers and complex problem solvers. Concurrently, it is our duty to the U.S. Army to also act as a "think factory" for commanders and civilian leaders at the strategic level worldwide and routinely engage in discourse and debate concerning the role of ground forces in achieving national security objectives.

The Strategic Studies Institute publishes national security and strategic research and analysis to influence policy debate and bridge the gap between military and academia.

The Center for Strategic Leadership contributes to the education of world class senior leaders, develops expert knowledge, and provides solutions to strategic Army issues affecting the national security community.

The Peacekeeping and Stability Operations Institute provides subject matter expertise, technical review, and writing expertise to agencies that develop stability operations concepts and doctrines.

The School of Strategic Landpower develops strategic leaders by providing a strong foundation of wisdom grounded in mastery of the profession of arms, and by serving as a crucible for educating future leaders in the analysis, evaluation, and refinement of professional expertise in war, strategy, operations, national security, resource management, and responsible command.

The U.S. Army Heritage and Education Center acquires, conserves, and exhibits historical materials for use to support the U.S. Army, educate an international audience, and honor Soldiers—past and present.

Strategic Studies Institute
and
U.S. Army War College Press

THE NORTH CAUCASUS INSURGENCY: DEAD OR ALIVE?

Emil Aslan Souleimanov

February 2017

*****

Comments pertaining to this report are invited and should be forwarded to: Director, Strategic Studies Institute and U.S. Army War College Press, U.S. Army War College, 47 Ashburn Drive, Carlisle, PA 17013-5010.

*****

Printed in the United States of America
ISBN: 978-1545325100

CONTENTS

FOREWORD

Violence in the North Caucasus, a multi-ethnic region on Europe's easternmost edge, has been going on almost continuously since 1994, becoming a hallmark of post-Soviet Russia. Back then, just 3 years after the dissolution of the Soviet Union and 5 years after the Soviet military's withdrawal from Afghanistan, armed conflict in the nation's southwestern periphery broke out following the Russian Army's incursion into the breakaway republic of Chechnya. Within less than a decade, what began as a local ethno-separatist rebellion effectively morphed into an Islamist insurgency, spreading in the early-2000s from Chechnya to most of the Muslim-majority region. Moreover, even though the Russian authorities declared in 2009 the ultimate end of the counterterrorist operation, jihadist groups have still been underway in the North Caucasus.

Against the background of impressive research on the political violence in the region, this monograph seeks to carefully evaluate the current situation and the prospects of the North Caucasus insurgency. To that end, it reviews the fundamental causes and the most-recent trends, both endogenous and exogenous, relating to the local insurgency. It explains in great detail the factors behind the unprecedented weakening of the local insurgency. At the same time, this monograph unveils the important shortcomings of these factors, pointing to the viability of the North

Caucasus insurgency and predicting that in the short and medium term, locally operating jihadist groups will remain a factor of regional and Russian politics.

Douglas C. Lovelace

DOUGLAS C. LOVELACE, JR.
Director
Strategic Studies Institute and
   U.S. Army War College Press

PREFACE

December 11, 2014, marked the 20th anniversary of Russia's first war in Chechnya. That war ended in a dramatic and decisive defeat for Russia.[1] Presently, fighting has died down in Chechnya, though it is still vulnerable to attacks, as we saw in late-2014.[2] However, more importantly, the conflict has spread to embrace virtually all of the North Caucasus, as Moscow fights a self-proclaimed jihadi organization, the Caucasus Emirate (CE). In other words, the present insurgency, and Russia's counterinsurgency, has gone on unabated for 20 years and shows no sign of stopping anytime soon. In this respect, the campaign in the North Caucasus bears considerable resemblance to other long-running wars across the Muslim world. Therefore, this war is not unlike the wars in Afghanistan and Iraq, in which the U.S. military has found itself enmeshed since 2001. However, the enormous outpouring of Western analyses of those wars and of insurgency and counterinsurgency seems, for the most part, to have bypassed the conflict or conflicts in the North Caucasus. Few studies, if any, incorporate these wars into their findings or use them as examples to confirm or to criticize one or another theory of insurgency or counterinsurgency that have developed over the last decade.

This monograph represents an initial attempt to rectify that oversight by focusing on one of the most-critical areas of study for the analysts of contemporary war; namely, the interaction between the counterinsurgents' armed forces and their operations on the one hand, and the culture (anthropologically-defined) and mores of the host population on the other hand. These mores, or manifestations of culture, are confined to neither religion, nationality, nor ethnicity, which are always slippery concepts in this part of the world. Rather, the cultural formations analyzed here relate to what anthropologists call "honor societies," which are founded on strong norms of honor, shame, and masculinity; namely, the codes of retaliation, silence, and hospitality. It is possible that these norms may have predated the Islamization of these societies, although by now they are thoroughly entwined with religion and concepts of ethnicity, if not national self-identification.

Indeed, this point marks the first time in this reviewer's knowledge that anyone has gone beyond the study of culture and religion to invoke or excavate these socio-anthropological categories as being major factors for recruitment, although students of other insurgencies who are regularly cited here have noted them in passing. This monograph, however, represents the first example of theory building, placing those concepts at the center of the analysis of motivations for recruitment of both insurgents and counterinsurgents. One hopes that this will lead to a series of further fruitful efforts to conduct a similar analysis of other wars. Moreover, this is also one of the first examples of the effort to conduct such a comparative analysis of the North Caucasus war in the light of Western theory. Robert Schaefer did this with regard to the principles of war for Chechnya; however, nobody has followed up on that endeavor.[3] Apart from Schaefer's systematic efforts at analyzing the wars in the North Caucasus empirically, other scholars' efforts, for all their undoubted merits, have eschewed either the comparative approach or the theory-building approach, or both.[4]

This comparative approach and effort to build theory is what makes this study particularly relevant to the U.S. Army and other branches of the U.S. Armed Forces. Given the new emphasis in the U.S. military of sensitizing troops to local cultures and mores, and even creating specially designated units of such forces, it becomes even more profitable, if not imperative, to view the Russian experience in the light of global manifestations of such wars and of the salience of such cultural values. For it is clear that these values or codes, to use the author's terminology, are not confined to the North Caucasus. For example, Arab societies in general appear to be very much caught up in these codes and are widely seen as honor societies or cultures. We see signs of this in the long-running wars between the Israelis and the Palestinians, if not in the earlier manifestations of this phenomenon in Israel's wars against the Arab states. Similarly, the well-known code of *omertà* in the Sicilian Mafia equates almost literally to the author's code of silence. Thus, Souleimanov has tapped into a rich vein of historical and societal thought that locates warlike behaviors in these codes — generally codes of masculinity — and finds them in societies as disparate as North Africa, the antebellum U.S. South, the contemporary Middle East, and southern Italy. Moreover, such confrontations between insurgents and counterinsurgents in these societies often are heavily influenced not only by the insurgents' behavior in terms of these codes, but also by the fact that in many cases, we are witnessing a so-called "war of national liberation" or a colony's uprising against a foreign occupier.[5] Moreover, in Western literature, as Albert Memmi observes, the trope for such behaviors may already be found in the relationship between Prospero and Caliban in Shakespeare's *The Tempest*.[6] As past and ongoing wars suggest, honor societies are not only tenacious in their defense of their values; they are also notoriously difficult places in which foreigners may try to establish durable and effective states or simply governing institutions.

What the author makes clear here is that despite 20 years of warfare, Moscow has not yet found the master key that would enable it to employ those codes for its own benefit. The exception is in Chechnya, where Moscow has been able to use the Kadyrov family — originally Father Akhmad, and after his murder, his son Ramzan — to "pacify" Chechnya. In general, Russia's ruthless, violent, and often criminal behavior has obstructed pacification of the North Caucasus and regularly affronted the naïve population's mores. As the author has found, Russia and Russian-led attacks upon these codes in Chechnya and the North Caucasus have facilitated recruitment into both the CE and the earlier Chechen movement; that was the original spark that ignited the wider current war. In this respect, the author's research and interviews appear to conform to the findings of much Western research into the conflicts of our time.

Indeed, the case of the Kadyrov family represents not just the need for establishing a political order that is responsive to those indigenous mores of these honor societies; it also evokes a recurrent pattern of Russian imperial history that is marked by hundreds of years of experience in imperial policing, empire-building, and thus, insurgency and counterinsurgency. Although we are simplifying drastically for reasons of space, there appear to be two broad paradigms that have been used, though not always with success, by Russian authorities, whether Tsarist, Soviet, or now, post-Soviet. To some degree, these paradigms are alternative strategies not usable in tandem. Rather, we often find that where the first direct, brutal assault upon the targeted society fails, it is replaced by a second, more indirect, and socio-politically sophisticated paradigm. However, there is some overlap in the tactics employed in either or both of these strategic paradigms. For example, deportation has been a major feature of both paradigms since it was first tried by Ivan III in 1478 against Novgorod. Nonetheless, for analytical purposes, we can distinguish between these two paradigms, especially in the North Caucasus.

The first of these strategic paradigms is one of brutal suppression and comprehensive direct assault on the enemy and its society. There are many examples: the Ermolov campaigns of brutal assaults on the people and mores of the North Caucasus in 1816-25, and those of similar provenance launched by his successors in the 1830-50s.[7] The most prominent recent examples are the collectivization struggle of 1929-33, where whole communities and peoples were deported or, as in Ukraine and Kazakhstan, subjected to famine; and Stalin's deportations of many nationalities, particularly in the North Caucasus in 1943-44.[8] Other such examples are the suppression of the Tambov peasant insurgency in 1920-21, which General Mikhail Tukhachevsky drowned in blood. To be sure, even in some of these dramas, e.g. collectivization, there were retreats and periods of concessions to the "insurgents." However, in the course of these wars, the brutal direct attack on people, and equally important, their way of life, is quite visible and the primary approach. Often, however, such responses were unavailable to Russian rulers, or the direct approach failed, forcing them to resort to alternative strategies.

Thus, the second paradigm attempts to combine a relatively more tailored or measured force (that is, relative in Russian terms of the time in question) with political and cultural-religious-economic concessions to the insurgents; the exploitation of indigenous values to achieve state objectives; or the incorporation, assimilation, or co-optation of elites—in this case the Kadyrov family, since Akhmad Kadyrov was the Mufti of Chechnya—who are willing to work with the Russian government. Common to the periods of a resort to this strategy is the fact that they generally occur in the context of a protracted campaign when the state is relatively weak, distracted by other contingencies, unsuccessful in its direct approach, or fully aware that size of the problem precludes the direct and brutal tactics of the previous strategy. In the North Caucasus, we see this particular strategy in play in 1920-21, when the Bolsheviks sought to consolidate their rule in the face of another of the periodic ethnoreligious uprisings against its authority, in the Second Chechen War of 1999-2007 (and during Ramzan Kadyrov's rule since then) and in the 1850s and 1860s in the North Caucasus against the legendary Shamil.[9] We also see it in the 1920s in Central Asia in Russia's attempt to suppress the Basmachi uprising when the direct approach had failed there.

Generally, this approach comes into play when it becomes clear that the direct and more brutal policy has failed and that something else must be tried. These concessions reflect a more sophisticated understanding and employment of the measures needed to undermine the cohesion and thus, the base of support for the insurgents by splitting the movement and balancing concession and appeals to indigenous values with repression. It is not only a question of making concessions to their way of life, nationality, and religion. It is quite consciously a strategy of imperial management, whose main component is to find those elites who are willing to work with Moscow or St. Petersburg, install them in leadership positions, co-opt them and their followers into the Russian ruling elite, which always was a cosmopolitan affair, make the requisite concessions to the people; and, over the long term, integrate these elites into the Russian state, thus depriving the population of a leadership stratum with which to lead any future revolts. Throughout the history of successful Russian imperial advances, we find either or both Moscow and St. Petersburg being able to rely quite successfully on the elites who form a pro-Russian party amidst targeted territories, peoples, and states.[10] Combined with overwhelming force and Moscow's ability — a common operational thread in all its ventures — to isolate the theater from foreign eyes and support, this blending of force and co-optation has generally proven successful, most recently in Chechnya.

Using the Kadyrovs, and the growing war-weari-ness of those left in Chechnya, Moscow was able to craft an appeal to Chechens that the insurgents, who had in fact succumbed to a Salafist and Saudi-inspired version of Islam, not unlike that espoused by Osama bin Laden and Ayman al-Zawahiri, were interlopers — outsiders who sought to hijack an indigenous Islamic theology for their own political purposes. Whether this development and promotion of religious schisms among the Chechens was a conscious Federal Secu-rity Service of the Russian Federation (FSB) strategy or a serendipitous exploitation of an opportunity that presented itself is irrelevant because the exploitation of this tactic fit so well with the evolving Russian strat-egy after the shameful defeat of 1996.[11]

Finally, as the insurgency weakened, Moscow was able to rely increasingly on the Kadyrovs and its policy of Chechenization buttressed by the *kadyrovtsy*'s (troops loyal to the Kadyrovs) and a massive infusion of capital for reinvestment or redevelopment of Chechnya, and the granting of enormous autonomous powers to Ramzan Kadyrov who has said he is Putin's man.[12] Here again, we see the dividends that accrue to Moscow from its ability to split the elite, namely, the ability to play what amounts to the amnesty card as many insurgents either think revolt is hopeless or that Kadyrov is achieving as much of the elite's former dream as is possible.

As the author points out, the *kadyrovtsy* were also successful and have remained successful despite their brutality because they invoke and respond to these same codes and are thus much more in harmony with the deep cultural structures of the local population. However, what has occurred in Chechnya has not happened in the North Caucasus and, as of 2014, there was no sign that Moscow would find answers to its problems anytime soon. Indeed, there is growing economic pressure being brought to bear on Russia. Moscow's ability to create viable economic opportunity in the North Caucasus and sustain it after 2015 will come under increasing strain from: imperial overstretch (the invasion, and now obligation, to support Crimea), Western sanctions, and the extinguishing of access to foreign capital; the huge decline in energy prices that strikes at Moscow's "cash crop" (the state's ability to gain income from energy); the depreciation of the ruble; and the huge structural problems attendant upon a kleptocratic, technologically uncompetitive, and backward economy. Meanwhile, the well-documented involvement of North Caucasian radicals in Syria, the Islamic State of Iraq and Syria (ISIS), and the fact of regular "commuting" of the men between theaters, suggests the potential for the ISIS threat to fuse with the CE just as the CE fused or affiliated with al-Qaeda a decade or more ago.

Consequently, we should not expect to see the end of violence in the North Caucasus any more than we should expect it to end in any of the theaters where it is not evidently deeply ensconced (e.g., Mali, Libya, Hamas, and Hezbollah in Gaza and Lebanon, Syria, Iraq, and Afghanistan). Under the circumstance, it should be clear that the fires burning in the North Caucasus resemble, if they are not identical to, those burning throughout the Middle East, Africa, and Afghanistan. In those cases, this monograph makes a significant contribution to the taxonomy of these movements and provides those who would study these wars, or who must prosecute them as counter-insurgents, with much food for productive thought.

Therefore, this is a provocative monograph that hopefully will open other analysts' eyes to the importance of these codes and sensitize U.S. and allied militaries to the need for an appreciation of the power and importance of these codes in current and, unfortunately, future wars.

DR. STEPHEN J. BLANK
Senior Fellow
American Foreign Policy
Council

ENDNOTES - PREFACE

1. A title like Anatol Lieven, *Chechnya: Tombstone of Russian Power*, New Haven, CT: Yale University Press, 1999, clearly captures that outcome.

2. Alexey Malashenko, "The Grozny Attack—What's Next?" Carnegie Moscow Center, December 11, 2014.

3. Robert W. Schaefer, *The Insurgency in Chechnya and the North Caucasus: From Gazavat to Jihad*, Santa Barbara, CA: Praeger Security International, 2011.

4. Gordon M. Hahn, *Russia's Islamic Threat*, New Haven, CT: Yale University Press, 2007, and subsequent writings cited in this monograph: Stephen J. Blank, "Russia's Ulster: The Chechen War and Its Consequences," Demokratizatsiya: The Journal of Post-Soviet Democratization, Vol. 9, No. 1, Winter 2001.

5. Albert Memmi, *The Colonizer and the Colonized*, expanded ed., Boston, MA: Beacon Press, 1991; Edward C. Banfield, *The Moral Basis of a Backward Society*, New York: The Free Press, 1967; Frantz Fanon, *The Wretched of the Earth*, New York: Grove Press, 2005; Bertram Wyatt-Brown, *The Shaping of Southern Culture: Honor, Grace, and War, 1760s-1890s*, Chapel Hill, NC: The University of North Carolina Press, 2001; Bertram Wyatt-Brown, *Honor and Violence in the Old South*, New York: Oxford University Press, 1986.

6. Memmi.

7. Moshe Gammer, "Russian Strategies in the Conquest of Chechnia and Daghestan, 1825-1859," in Marie Bennigsen Broxup, ed., *The North Caucasus Barrier: the Russian Advance Towards the Muslim World*, New York: St. Martin's Press, 1992, pp. 45-61.

8. For recent accounts, see Timothy Snyder, *Bloodlands: Europe Between Hitler and Stalin*, New York: Basic Books, 2010; Norman M. Naimark, *Stalin's Genocides*, Princeton, NJ: Princeton University Press, 2010.

9. Schaefer; and Stephen Blank, "The Formation of the Soviet North Caucasus, 1918-24," *Central Asian Survey*, Vol. 12,

No. 1, 1993, pp. 13-32; Alfred J. Rieber, ed., *The Politics of Autocracy: Letters of Alexander II to Prince A. I. Bariatinskii, 1857-1864,* Paris: Mouton, 1966.

10. For example, see John P. LeDonne, *The Grand Strategy of the Russian Empire 1650-1831,* New York: Oxford University Press, 2004.

11. Schaefer, pp. 170-172.

12. Svante E. Cornell, "The 'Afghanization' of the North Caucasus: Causes and Implications of a Changing Conflict," in Stephen J. Blank, ed., *Russia's Homegrown Insurgency: Jihad in the North Caucasus,* Carlisle, PA: Strategic Studies Institute, U.S. Army War College, 2012.

ABOUT THE AUTHOR

EMIL ASLAN SOULEIMANOV is an associate professor of political science at the Department of Security Studies, Institute of Political Science, Faculty of Social Sciences, Charles University in Prague, Czech Republic. Dr. Souleimanov's current research focuses on the political ethnography of insurgency and counterinsurgency in Russia's North Caucasus. He is the co-author of *The Individual Disengagement of Avengers, Nationalists, and Jihadists* (with Huseyn Aliyev, Palgrave Macmillan, 2014) and *Understanding Ethnopolitical Conflict: Karabakh, South Ossetia, and Abkhazia Wars Reconsidered* (Palgrave Macmillan, 2013). His work has appeared or is forthcoming in *International Security, World Politics, International Politics, Journal of Strategic Studies, Terrorism and Political Violence, Post-Soviet Affairs, Europe-Asia Studies, Middle East Policy,* and others.

SUMMARY

Since the mid-1990s, Chechnya and the North Caucasus have attracted the attention of policymakers, scholars, and experts interested in the theory and practice of separatism, insurgency, and terrorism. As a natural laboratory of political violence in its most distinct forms, the North Caucasus, with inherent ethnic divisions, religious radicalism, an intricate sociocultural profile, and uneasy center-periphery relationships, has been a source of impressive scholarship. While a lot has been written on the causes and contexts of the North Caucasus insurgency, a consensus is still to be reached in the academic and expert community as to the structural factors leading to violent mobilization and pro-insurgent support in Russia's volatile region. Moreover, the recent trend of weakening insurgent groups operating in the North Caucasus remains largely unexplored.

This monograph builds on and expands the extant scholarship. Specifically, it contributes to the general understanding of the root causes of the regional insurgency and its recent developments. The monograph points to the necessity of comprehending both dimensions in order to evaluate the viability of the North Caucasus insurgency.

First, it sorts out the plethora of studies on the structural causes of the violent mobilization in Russia's most multi-ethnic region, categorizing them along the lines of three main approaches: Chechnya and North Caucasus as a battleground of global Salafi jihad; individual grievances; and, protest to social injustice and the erosion of traditional values. This monograph refers to the most up-to-date ethnographic research in the field that points to the salience of individual and collective grievances. Due to the culture of honor, many young North Caucasians have sought to join insurgent groups for the sake of revenge, largely irrespective of political or ideological motivations. This indicates that the North Caucasus insurgency has been, from its very beginning, a homegrown phenomenon. Subsequently, the monograph categorizes the scholarship on the causes of pro-insurgent support, a heavily under-researched field in both theoretical and empirical literature. It identifies two main competing approaches explaining pro-insurgent support: greed and sociocultural codes. This monograph also points to the crucial importance, underexplored in previous research, of the sociocultural codes of hospitality and silence. It illustrates that these codes, embedded in the local cultural tradition, have prompted part of the local population to provide support to the insurgents in spite of the risk of severe punishment at the hand of the incumbent power holder.

The second part of the monograph focuses on the recent trends in the regional insurgency. First, combining primary and secondary data, it identifies four main factors that have since the early-2010s led to the gradual decline of the North Caucasus insurgency. The first factor leading to a decline of the insurgency is the selective targeting by Russian and local counterinsurgents of the insurgents' local support base, including the insurgents' relatives. Over time, this controversial practice, well-proved in Chechnya in the early-2000s, has prompted many locals across the North Caucasus to withhold support from the insurgents. The second factor leading to a decline of the insurgency is the deployment of elite counterinsurgent forces and army units in special operations, and the withdrawal of counterinsurgency operations from local police forces known for their incompetence and corruption. The third factor leading to a decline of the insurgency is the infiltration by counterinsurgent agents of insurgent groups, resulting in their subsequent decapitation. Since early-2010, this method has led to the substantial weakening of the locally operating jihadist groups, because the loss of experienced leaders sufficiently affected the jihadists' capability to operate effectively. The fourth factor leading to the decline of the insurgency is the volunteering of thousands of North Caucasians to fight in the Syrian Civil War away from their native region. The monograph shows that internal disputes that plagued the numerous factions of the Caucasus Emirate (CE), a loosely organized group, have prompted thousands of North Caucasians to travel to Syria. This, in turn, has reduced the share of prospective recruits to the locally operating insurgent groups.

Having explained the factors behind the unprecedented weakening of the North Caucasus insurgency in the recent years, the monograph moves on to explore the important shortcomings of these factors. First, despite severe penalization at the hand of the incumbents in compliance with the locally embedded sociocultural codes of retaliation, hospitality, and silence, a segment of the North Caucasian population has still joined insurgent groups or provided support to them. As long as the incumbent forces continue to target the local population, avengers will recruit in order to restore individual and family honor. Despite important setbacks experienced by local insurgent groups in recent years, these structural causes have remained intact. Second, with elite Russian forces, famed for their low numbers, deployed in the distant battlefields of Eastern Ukraine's Donbas and Syria, the burden of fighting the local insurgency has again largely fallen onto the shoulders of the local police and minor counterterrorist units. This has recently reduced the overall effectiveness of counterinsurgent and counterterrorist operations in the North Caucasus. Moreover, while the current situation enables the local counterinsurgent forces to face the weakened insurgent groups, this monograph shows that in the short and medium term, the situation may reverse should the insurgency be bolstered by new waves of recruits. Fourth, many frustrated North Caucasians have recently grown disillusioned with the "Syrian Jihad" in general and the Islamic State in particular. Therefore, they have sought to stay in their native region. In the short term, this may lead to an increase in the number of North Caucasians recruited to the locally operating jihadist groups, invigorating the regional insurgency.

THE NORTH CAUCASUS INSURGENCY: DEAD OR ALIVE?

On April 16, 2009, then-President Dmitry Medvedev announced the much-anticipated end of the counterterrorist operation in Chechnya, an autonomous republic in the North Caucasus along Russia's restless southwestern border. The country's Counterterrorist Committee declared an immediate end to all military operations in Chechnya, with thousands of Russian troops set to leave the troublesome republic within weeks. Public opinion considered this a personal victory for Vladimir Putin, who came to power and subsequently strengthened his grip over the country as a gifted statesman and strategist, capable of eliminating the threat of terrorism and insurgency. Ramzan Kadyrov, Chechnya's strongman and Putin's close ally, boasted to the Russian media: "We are extremely satisfied. The modern Chechen Republic is a peaceful and budding territory. The end of the counterterrorist operation will spur on economic growth in the republic."[1] At the time, this statement was considered a milestone by many in Russia, because of its state-controlled media. It appeared that the violence that had plagued the North Caucasus almost incessantly since the mid-1990s had at last come to an end.

However, not all shared the optimism of Russian and Chechen elites. Grigory Shvedov, a liberal Russian journalist and expert on the North Caucasus, stated at the time that "the number of bombings, terrorist attacks and murders as in the past remains high; they occur every week. It is a fairy tale that Chechnya has become a stable region."[2] Others located both within and outside of Russia, who were knowledgeable about

1

the situation on the ground in the North Caucasus, also challenged the mainstream viewpoint, while still acknowledging a certain improvement in Chechnya. However, these voices went unheard in Russia.

While Russian troops, aided by their Chechen proxies, managed to gain relative control over the situation in Chechnya—the former epicenter of insurgent violence in the North Caucasus—things soon deteriorated elsewhere in the region. Since approximately the end of 2009 to the beginning of 2010, insurgency-related violence has skyrocketed across the entire North Caucasus region. Dagestan, Ingushetia, and Kabardino-Balkaria emerged as new hotbeds of insurgency, eclipsing Chechnya.[3] Local jihadist groups started making inroads into North Ossetia, a predominantly Orthodox republic in the North Caucasus, and into Karachayevo-Cherkesiya, a significantly Russified autonomous republic far from the established hotbeds of insurgent violence in the Northeastern Caucasus.[4] According to some reports, North Caucasian insurgents went so far as to establish connections in Russia's Muslim-dominated Volga-Ural region as well.[5] According to Ivan Sydoruk, Deputy Prosecutor General of the North Caucasus Federal District, the region witnessed a 300 percent increase in "serious terrorist attacks" during the first 8 months of 2010, compared to the same period in 2009.[6] In August 2012 alone, at least 182 registered deaths related to the ongoing insurgency were reported in the North Caucasus, and at least 100 deaths on average were reported every single month from the region in the same year.[7]

Moreover, violence did not remain confined to the borders of Russia's North Caucasus republics. In March 2010, two crowded subway stations in Moscow were targeted by suicide bombers, resulting in the deaths of 40 civilians. In January 2011, a bomb exploded in Moscow's busy Domodedovo International Airport, leaving 37 dead. In 2013, three suicide bombings on October 21, December 29, and December 30, shook Volgograd, an important city on the Volga River, leaving a total of 41 dead and dozens injured.[8] In addition, dozens of violent attacks aimed at civilians, law enforcement officials (*siloviki*), and pro-regime authorities occurred across Russia proper and the North Caucasus. It increasingly appeared that, rather than winning a war against terrorists, the country was instead being engulfed by waves of violence. The early-2010s also saw Dagestan, a multi-ethnic autonomous republic on the shores of the Caspian Sea that had been a rather peaceful area in previous years, turn into the nucleus of the North Caucasus insurgency.[9]

Since 2014, however, the North Caucasus jihadist insurgency has undergone an abrupt turnaround. Between 2013 and 2014, insurgency-related violence decreased by around 47 percent, thereby marking the most abrupt decrease in violence in the history of the regional insurgency. In absolute numbers, only 37 civilians were killed in 2014, a sharp decrease compared to 104 civilian casualties in 2013. While 424 *siloviki* were killed in 2013, the number decreased by nearly half, to 221 deaths, the following year. While North Caucasian jihadists carried out 100 detonations in 2013, this figure shrank to less than 25 in 2014. On the other hand, only 248 insurgents were killed in 2014, as a consequence of counterinsurgent raids, in comparison to 298 in 2013.[10]

Despite the decline in violence discussed above, insurgency-related violence in the North Caucasus appears to be gaining momentum once again. In 2014, the number of casualties (52 killed and 65 injured) rose by 15.8 percent from 2013, with most casualties taking place in the last quarter of 2014.[11] By mid-2015, 77 people had been killed in the North Caucasus.[12] These figures only show a slight change; therefore, they should be taken cautiously, but do attest to Russia's failure to completely wipe out the regional insurgency, as frequently claimed by Russian authorities.[13] In the short term, these oscillating figures may indicate a reversion to more insurgency-related violence in the region conditioned by a slow rise of the North Caucasian insurgency.

Importantly, a consolidated attack in December 2014 revived doubts about the alleged elimination of Chechen insurgent groups that was frequently boasted by Russian authorities.[14] At that time, around 20 Chechen insurgents executed a surprise attack in Grozny, and having ambushed a unit of Chechen special police—known as the *kadyrovtsy*—on the outskirts of Grozny, the insurgents penetrated into the city center and seized an important administrative building. According to official reports, 14 pro-Moscow Chechen police officers were killed as a result of the intense fighting, and most of the attackers appear to have died. Against the background of the December 2014 attack in Grozny, Mairbek Vatchagaev claims that harsh acts of retaliatory violence notwithstanding, around 100 Chechen insurgents still operate in Chechnya's wooded mountains.[15] There are several hundred insurgents in the neighboring republic of Dagestan, with dozens of insurgents also still active in Ingushetia and Kabardino-Balkaria.[16] Triumphant reports from federal and local authorities about the ultimate defeat of the local jihadist underground are contrasted with periodic news resurfacing in the media of liquidating important insurgent leaders and their groups, as in the case of presumably successful counterterrorist operations carried out in Kabardino-Balkaria and Dagestan in late-August of 2016.[17]

Having declared victory over the North Caucasus insurgency, in general, Russian authorities have endeavored to remain silent on the recent incidents of insurgency-related violence in the North Caucasus, and in Chechnya in particular. For example, Chechen and federal media chose not to report on a bomb blast in Grozny on February 26, 2015.[18] When five Russian service members from the Ministry of Interior's Special Forces were severely wounded in a bomb blast in Chechnya's Urus-Martan district, the incident was given virtually no coverage in Chechen and Russian media outlets.[19] On August 8, 2015, the Russian commander of a paratrooper unit and two service members were wounded in the wooded terrain of Chechnya's Achkhoy-Martan district after stepping on an anti-personnel mine. In contrast to the widely publicized reports on liquidated insurgents and their leaders, this news received virtually no federal coverage.[20] Despite the silence, the Russian authorities do appear to be concerned about the North Caucasus insurgency's ability to inflict sensitive blows. According to a statement in February 2015 by Sergey Ivanov, Chief of Staff of the Presidential Administration of Russia, the situation in parts of the North Caucasus remains tense, with the "number of [terrorist and insurgent] crimes having increased since last year [2014]."[21] The latest developments illustrate that, despite long-standing counterinsurgency efforts, the insurgency in the region has survived.

During the period from 2013–2014, the North Caucasus insurgency experienced a sharp decline in violent activity, a decline that superseded its peak in the early-2010s. The statistics in 2014, nevertheless, show a slight increase in insurgency-related violence, particularly in Dagestan—the most populous republic of the North Caucasus and the leader of the regional insurgency.

What explains the decline of insurgency-related violence during the period 2013–2014, and what factors are to be held accountable for the recent rise in insurgency-related violence? Is the North Caucasus insurgency on the brink of extinction, given Russia's immense superiority in military, economic, and demographic resources?

This monograph offers a comprehensive analysis of the developments in the North Caucasus insurgency since 2013. It claims that the main counterinsurgency methods of selectively targeting insurgents and their supporters, collective punishment of insurgents' relatives, and infiltration and decapitation of insurgent groups currently deployed in the North Caucasus—and particularly in Dagestan—are rooted in Russia's relatively successful counterinsurgency campaign in Chechnya, conducted from the mid-2000s to around 2010. In addition, the monograph analyzes the impact that the departure of hundreds of North Caucasian volunteers to Syria to participate in the local jihad has had on the North Caucasian insurgency. This monograph also offers insight into the microcosm of the North Caucasus insurgency and counterinsurgency to examine the vicissitudes of the ongoing violence in Russia's troublesome border region in the broader context of the sources of violent mobilization and pro-insurgent support. Identifying the causes of violent mobilization and pro-insurgent support is crucial for the survival of any insurgency. This monograph traces the impact of Moscow's recent counterinsurgency policies on individual fighters' determination to mobilize and the local population's willingness or reluctance to support insurgents. In so doing, the monograph examines the key sources of the North Caucasian insurgency that are tied to its long-term viability.

Unlike the prevalent macro-level work on the regional insurgency that has evolved around the notions of history, ideology, and repression, this monograph treats insurgent activity as a dynamic process that hinges on local support and is responsive to the incumbents' use of indiscriminate or selective violence. It looks into the key sources of the North Caucasus insurgency, particularly the persistence of semi-archaic sociocultural codes of retaliation, hospitality, and silence that ensure violent mobilization and pro-insurgency support, even in the face of acts of retaliation by adversaries. The monograph concludes that, despite considerable setbacks recently experienced by regional insurgent groups, the North Caucasus insurgency is likely to survive in the years to come.

The monograph is divided into four main sections: the first section serves as the introduction and consists of a portrayal of the North Caucasus, a region largely unknown to the western readership. This section emphasizes the history of armed conflict and insurgency, the ethnography of the region—namely the persisting social hierarchy and norms that have shaped the violence in the region—and the region's current socioeconomic and political circumstances. The major causes of violent mobilization and pro-insurgent support in the North Caucasus are categorized and critically evaluated by drawing from elaborate scholarship on the topic. The second section deals with the Russian counterinsurgency in Chechnya during the 2000–2010 time period, and scrutinizes the sources of Russia's relatively effective counterinsurgency in the troublesome republic: the deployment of selective targeting against insurgents and their supporters; collective punishment of the insurgents' relatives with the aim of deterring prospective insurgents from joining insurgent groups; and, infiltration and decapitation of Chechen insurgent groups. The third section then analyzes the impact of these counterinsurgency methods — previously deployed in Chechnya — on the North Caucasus insurgency and the rest of the North Caucasus, particularly in Dagestan, a hotbed of the regional insurgency. While the initial part of this section focuses on the relative successes of these methods, the second part casts light on the shortcomings of them. The fourth section summarizes the findings of this monograph.

I. INTRODUCING THE NORTH CAUCASUS

The North Caucasus is a predominantly mountainous region stretching from the Black Sea to the Caspian Sea, located north of the Greater Caucasus mountain range and constituting Europe's natural geographical border with Asia. Inhabited by dozens of indigenous ethnic groups, the region has historically been considered a Babylon of languages.[22] Sunni Islam is currently the main religion of most indigenous North Caucasian ethnic groups, with the exceptions of the predominantly Orthodox North Ossetians, and a small population of minority Shiite Lezgins and Judaic Tats in the southernmost region of Dagestan.[23] The North Caucasus is also home to a strong Russian minority, particularly in the central (North Ossetia) and western (Kabardino-Balkaria and Karachayevo-Cherkesiya) areas. With the exception of the Russian-dominated Stavropol and Krasnodar provinces, what is commonly referred to as the North Caucasus[24] is divided into six ethnic autonomous republics (from east to west): Dagestan, Chechnya, Ingushetia, North Ossetia, Kabardino-Balkaria, and Karachayevo-Cherkesiya. The collective population of these republics is less than seven million.

A HISTORY OF REBELLIONS

The region served as a battleground of insurgency from the late-18th century to the mid-19th century. Facing an invading Russian army, a series of rebellions broke out in the region—which was dominated by village communities and small principalities—and turned into what came to be known as the Caucasian

War—the longest protracted war in Russian history.[25] Periodic uprisings continued to occur even after the backbone of the highlanders' resistance was broken during the period between 1859 and 1864, particularly in the eastern parts of the region, which preserved their genuine ethno-demographic makeup.[26] The last hotbed of anti-Soviet resistance was quelled in Chechnya's mountains as late as the 1940s, with the Chechen population (along with the Ingush and Karachay-Balkars) deported *en masse* to Central Asia on the pretext of their collaboration with the Nazis.

Following World War II, autonomous republics existed in the North Caucasus, and the deported populations were allowed to return to their homeland in the second half of the 1950s. In the late-1980s, following the unprecedented détente, separatist aspirations strengthened among some North Caucasian ethnic groups, particularly the Chechens. The Russian army entered Chechnya in 1994, following a 3-year period of Chechen de facto independence. As Russian and Chechen elites were unable to negotiate Chechnya's status as part of the Russian Federation, a war ensued that claimed the lives of dozens of thousands of people, mostly Chechen civilians.[27] Severely unpopular in Russia, the war ultimately ended in 1996 with Russian troops pulling out of the troublesome republic. At the time, this move was widely considered to be Moscow's acknowledgment of its military defeat to an adversary, which was one million people-strong, as well as a source of shame for Russian nationalists.[28]

Following a 3-year *intermezzo*, the war resurfaced with the Chechen-Dagestani jihadist incursion into Dagestan's eastern areas in August of 1999, along with a subsequent wave of terrorist bombings in Russian cities. Attributed—falsely, as it turned out—to

Chechen jihadists as a form of retaliation for their failed incursion into Dagestan, these terrorist bombings generated widespread outrage across Russian society. Soon thereafter, Russian troops marched into Chechnya in the fall of 1999, marking the beginning of what came to be known as the Second Russo-Chechen War.[29] Grozny was retaken by the Russian army by March 2000, and by the early-2000s, Russian troops, aided by pro-Moscow Chechen paramilitary units known as the *kadyrovtsy*, largely held sway over Chechnya. The conflict was not limited to Chechnya, however, and quickly spread across the North Caucasus. This was particularly demonstrated by a series of raids conducted by local insurgent groups on Ingushetia's then-capital city Nazran (June 2004), Kabardino-Balkaria's capital city Nalchik (October 2005), and the increasingly impudent insurgent and terrorist attacks and assassinations in Dagestan.

Large-scale use of violence against true or alleged Salafis across the region in the wake of the 1999 bombings, reinforced by the 9/11 attacks in the United States, all led to the radicalization of local, predominantly peaceful, Salafi communities,[30] and also contributed to the emergence of hundreds of non-Salafi avengers.[31] In 2007, the leadership of the separatist Chechen Republic of Ichkeria proclaimed the establishment of the Caucasus Emirate (CE), a virtual theocracy based on the rule of Islamic law.[32]

Despite having virtually no control on the ground, the CE lays claim to the vast area of the North Caucasus for its domain.[33] At the time, this move was interpreted as the Chechen jihadist leadership's efforts to spread the armed conflict across the region, capitalizing on the grievances of the North Caucasian population.[34]

ETHNOGRAPHIC PROFILE

The North Caucasus historically has been considered a socially conservative region, partly due to the mountainous region's isolation from the rest of the world. The eastern republics of Chechnya, Dagestan, and Ingushetia constituted some of the most traditionalist areas of the former Soviet Union. A number of important socioeconomic changes occurred in the decades following World War II, and many highlanders moved down to urban areas or the cities of Russia proper. Although urbanization, modernization, and the influx of a large Russian-speaking population have somewhat reduced the scale of traditionalism in the region, it persists to this day.

Ingushetia, Chechnya, and, to a lesser extent, Dagestan, are clan societies, with individuals in these republics usually conceived of as members of a particular clan.[35] These republics' strong sense of clan-based solidarity affects a variety of social practices, such as retaliation, and forms of collective responsibility or punishment.[36] In Ingushetia and Chechnya, and to a lesser degree, in the heavily mountainous areas of Central and Western Dagestan, the custom of blood revenge still persists. Revolving around the notion of honor, this custom dictates that a male who has suffered an offense in the form of a grave insult—such as the killing or injuring of his relatives or rape of a female relative—is expected to retaliate by his fellow community members. Retaliation may be directed either against the direct culprit of the offense or, in the case that he cannot be reached, against the culprit's male relatives.[37] Collective responsibility and punishment have therefore been considered legitimate social practices in Ingushetia and Chechnya. Retaliation may be carried out either by the "offended" male himself, if he has survived the offense, or by his male relatives. Retaliation usually urges counter-retaliation, as members of the affected family or clan also want to exact retaliation on the offenders in order to avoid public disdain. This leads to a vicious circle of violence, with blood feuds lasting for generations. While the tradition of blood feuds has largely faded away in the rest of the North Caucasus, the code of retaliation still endures.

The code of hospitality guided the lives of highlanders for centuries and dictates that its adherents care for those in need. While this includes both insiders and outsiders, North Caucasians — bound by the principle of a clan or neighborhood-based solidarity — have prioritized support to insiders over outsiders. Historically, the code of hospitality has applied to *abreks* — avengers or outlaws — who have challenged the Russian authorities and, to a lesser extent, the local nobility that are perceived as allied with the Russian colonizers.[38] To this day, the local population considers the provision of support to insurgents fighting against the unjust, repressive, and corrupt system associated with the authorities to be a matter of honor.[39]

The code of silence, similar to the southern Italian custom of *omertà*, discourages the highlanders from discussing their internal affairs with outsiders and instead to resolve issues internally. Collaboration with the authorities or law enforcement is discouraged, even if one's life, property, or honor is at stake. Individuals are instead expected to resolve their troubles on their own, and "complaining" is considered behavior unworthy of a highlander.[40]

The natives of the North Caucasus are famous in Russia for their strong, socially conservative, and traditionalist views. This has manifested itself particularly in the North Caucasians' negative stance toward homosexuality—a controversial issue in Russia—as well as female emancipation, drug abuse, and other phenomena considered by many, particularly in the Northeast Caucasus, to constitute a dangerous erosion of the local population's age-old values. In general, the eastern North Caucasus is more socially conservative than the rest of the region, with rural and particularly isolated wooded mountainous areas more conservative than urban areas.[41]

SOCIOECONOMIC AND POLITICAL SITUATION

Although indicators vary across the region, the North Caucasus is among Russia's poorest regions.[42] Historically, unemployment rates have been high in the region, and according to independent estimates, around 80 percent of Chechnya's population was unemployed in 2014.[43] In Ingushetia, a tiny republic of 3,000 square kilometers, official sources place the number of unemployed individuals at around 31 percent.[44] In Kabardino-Balkaria, the number stood at around 18.3 percent in 2014, followed by Dagestan at 13.4 percent.[45] Unemployment is extremely high among youth and those in the heavily mountainous areas of the Northeast Caucasus, which has pushed thousands of Chechens, Ingush, and Dagestanis to travel to Russian cities outside of the region in search of jobs and better lives. While Chechnya's economic decline may be, at least partially, attributed to the two wars and lasting counterinsurgency that have beset the region since the mid-1990s, the dramatic state of Dagestan and Kabardino-Balkaria's economies are largely a result of the dissolution of the Soviet Union and the ensuing decline of the republic's industry, which was part of the Soviet centralized economy. A former hub of regional industry, Dagestan currently falls in the middle of Russia's 83 federal subjects in terms of its gross regional product (GRP), while it is ranked 70th on the list of Russia's federal subjects by gross domestic product (GDP) per capita, followed by Ingushetia and Kabardino-Balkaria,[46] and with Chechnya 79th, in terms of its GDP. As a result, all North Caucasian republics are heavily subsidized by Moscow, with federal transfers accounting for around 70 to 80 percent of these republics' budgets.[47] Against this background, natural demographic growth has ranked among the highest in Chechnya and Dagestan, together with Ingushetia.[48]

In addition to its difficult economic circumstances, the North Caucasus is notorious for corruption, which is unprecedented even by Russian standards. Decrying this state of affairs, then-President Medvedev went so far as to call it "monstrous."[49] According to Dagestani sources, no government job could be obtained without bribery,[50] and in a recent survey, 71 percent of Dagestani respondents associated the escalation of violence with the republic's endemic problems of unemployment and corruption.[51] Dagestan is no exception in this regard, with similar attitudes prevalent in other republics throughout the region.

The region is also known for its strong ethnic nationalism, which manifests itself particularly in the ethnically heterogeneous republics of Dagestan and Kabardino-Balkaria. Dagestan is home to 3 million inhabitants and 14 major indigenous ethnic groups, each divided into a considerably larger number of subethnic groups and clans or *tukhums,* territorially defined groups of *teips.* Importantly, none of these 14 major ethnic groups forms a majority, and the largest ethnic community — the Avars — make up less than one-third of the republic's entire population. Dagestan is often referred to as a consociational republic, in which ethnic demography translates into political dominance. Districts in which one ethnic community forms a majority are governed by representatives of that same ethnic community.[52] Given the ethnic favoritism and nepotism that Dagestan is notorious for, this situation magnifies the extent to which members of the ethnic community dominating a given area control its political and economic spheres. This naturally creates tension across the republic, with members of demographically weaker ethnic communities considering themselves to be discriminated against by their demographically stronger fellow Dagestanis. Interestingly, many Dagestanis have opposed the figure of the republic's president, usually an Avar, on the grounds that he represents a competing ethnic group.[53]

While Chechnya and Ingushetia are today largely mono-ethnic, a situation similar to that of Dagestan has existed in Kabardino-Balkaria, a republic of less than 900,000 inhabitants. Due to the demographic dominance of the Kabardin majority, which makes up around 57 percent of the republic's population, the republic's economy and politics have been largely dominated by the Kabardins, much to the dissatisfaction of the minority Balkars, who make up less than 13 percent of the republic's population.[54] In the past, this has led Turcophone Balkars to seek an autonomous republic of their own.

UNDERSTANDING THE CAUSES OF INSURGENT MOBILIZATION IN THE NORTH CAUCASUS

The Global Jihadism Paradigm.

Three major approaches have dominated the debate on the causes of insurgent violence in the North Caucasus. In an effort to link the regional insurgency to the phenomenon of global jihad, one of these approaches postulates that in general, the regional insurgency is a product of religious fanaticism and Salafi-jihadist ideology in particular. This approach maintains that the phenomenon was either imported to Russia, or inspired and supported from outside of Russia.[55] An eminent advocate of this approach, Gordon Hahn, argues that the "Chechens' radicalization [happened] under the influence of foreign, jihadist terrorist ideologies and movements funded, inspired and perhaps still coordinated by Al Qaeda."[56] Indeed, Russian authorities began to point out Chechen insurgents' intimate links to al-Qaeda (and the Taliban) in the immediate aftermath of the 9/11 attacks. According to Russian diplomats, dozens of Chechens in the service of the Taliban took part in the Afghanistan war against coalition forces in 2001; however, it was soon revealed that rumors of Chechens fighting in the ranks of the Taliban or captured by the Americans were ungrounded.[57] Russian authorities and state-owned media expounded on the thesis, maintaining that Osama bin Laden and Mullah Omar — the Taliban's mysterious commander — were hiding in the mountains of Chechnya following the crackdown on the Taliban by the U.S.-led coalition.[58]

17

According to the proponents of this approach, once Salafi-jihadist ideology spread among the ranks of Chechen insurgents, it soon expanded across the whole of the North Caucasus—a process that gained momentum in the late-1990s and particularly in the early-2000s.[59] Against this background, the establishment of the CE in 2007, which marked the definite decline of the Chechen nationalist project, is seen as a logical outcome of the spread of Salafi-jihadism in the region; the Chechen and North Caucasians' growing connections with al-Qaeda; and the role of transnational jihadist fighters in Chechnya and the region.[60] An important subdivision of this approach focuses on the phenomenon of transnational jihadists as an important source of jihadization of the local—initially ethno-nationalist—insurgency. During and after the First Chechen War (1994–1996), dozens of Arab veterans of the Soviet-Afghan War (1979–1989), who were experienced jihadists, took part in the hostilities in the North Caucasus. Some of these individuals, such as the Saudi-born *amir* Khattab, asserted themselves as leading figures of the Chechen insurgency.

During the First Chechen War and the interwar period (1996–1999), these jihadist leaders gradually radicalized a generation of Chechen fighters and frustrated North Caucasian youth. Yossef Bodansky claims that it was the influx of Arab jihadists traveling to Chechnya in the second half of the 1990s and their support from Persian Gulf monarchies that prompted the jihadization of the Chechen insurgency movement. The present-day North Caucasus insurgency is thus considered a phenomenon that largely lacks local roots.[61]

This assertion is not without merit, as local insurgents have presented themselves and their armed struggle as an increasingly religious affair that has been shaped by Salafi-jihadist principles and aims since at least the early-2000s. Following a gradual process of Islamization, the Chechen insurgents had fully adopted Salafi-jihadist ideology by 2007. Their organization and methods of warfare became increasingly reminiscent of al-Qaeda-affiliated groups. Consequently, the Chechen Republic of Ichkeria — a predominantly ethno-nationalist separatist movement — was replaced with the CE, a virtual and supra-ethnic theocracy adhering to Salafi-jihadism.[62]

While the proponents of the global jihadism paradigm prevail in Russia,[63] they have been widely criticized in Western academic and expert circles on a variety of grounds. For example, Jean-François Ratelle observes that:

> The claims made in these books are rarely supported with any footnotes or references and rely on unsupported and irrefutable claims by the authors. In the rare cases when they are, the sources are rather unreliable and vague, apparently trying to conceal the fact that these authors are presenting their conjectural opinions rather than academic analysis.[64]

A number of authors have challenged the Islamization, or more accurately, the jihadization of the Chechen and North Caucasus insurgency as a process caused predominantly or exclusively by exogenous influences. Matthew Evangelista, Julie Wilhelmsen, and Ekaterina Sokirianskaya have pointed to the superficial use of religious symbols and rhetoric by Chechen political and military elites to legitimize their non-religious claims in a society that regards Islam as the ultimate source of legitimacy.[65] The present author points to the example of the jihadization of the anti-regime Chechen elites, led by the infamous warlord Shamil Basayev, in interwar Chechnya, as a means of compromising and thwarting the secular regime of their former President, Aslan Maskhadov.[66] The rise of political Islam, including Salafi-jihadism, is not proof of external influences as such; rather, religious identity, together with secular identities based on ethnicity and kinship, became entrenched against the backdrop of armed conflict. When overly politicized, religious identity guides violent mobilization in conflict, while ethnic and kinship bonds constitute momentous forms of social capital.[67]

Ethnographic work provides valuable insight into the homegrown nature of jihadization in the North Caucasus. For example, the present author has illustrated that, against the backdrop of post-war Chechnya during 1996–1999, when members of weak clans were discriminated against by members of stronger clans, the weaker clans eventually sought to enter the locally operating Salafi-jihadist groups in order to ensure their own security and that of their relatives. Others determined to retaliate, but unable to do so on their own, joined jihadist groups in order to have the support of similarly-minded comrades-in-arms.[68] Many were determined to retaliate to avenge the death of a relative or close person, or a personal humiliation such as rape. As these individuals were only able to retaliate through self-sacrifice in the form of a suicide terrorist attack, they instead turned to religion to rationalize what they came to consider an act of martyrdom. Jihadization therefore constituted part of their reconciliation with the idea of retaliation by means of self-sacrifice.[69] Since the early-2000s, many disenfranchised North Caucasians have sought membership in jihadist groups, which for them constitutes the sole challenger to the unpopular local regimes (which had brought about the eradication of secular political opposition in the North Caucasus), and an unparalleled anti-establishment force.[70] Some individuals have joined jihadist groups to protest social injustice or the erosion of traditionalist values.[71] Others, already radicalized by a previous personal trigger — such as abuse, a perception of injustice, or humiliation — turned to Salafi-jihadism to justify their violent mobilization in their own eyes.[72] Triggered by an act of offense and hoping to retaliate, they underwent already-violent mobilization without being initially influenced by Salafi-jihadism. Over time, having entered jihadist groups, most of these individuals came to truly believe and self-identify with their group's ideology — in this case, the ideology of Salafi-jihadism.[73]

In addition, Ratelle notes that, despite numerous allegations by the proponents of the global jihadism approach, there is no solid evidence of the Chechen or North Caucasian's alliance with al-Qaeda, their participation in Taliban groups in Afghanistan and Pakistan, or other such groups.[74] While the role in the Chechen insurgency's jihadization in the late-1990s played by Arabs who previously participated in the Russo-Afghan War is disputed,[75] there is a widespread consensus that the North Caucasus has not had foreign fighters on its soil in recent years.[76] The argument that the jihadization of the Chechen and North Caucasian insurgencies was driven by religious fervor or the appeal of Salafi-jihadist doctrine has also been challenged as unsubstantiated.[77] In keeping with the prevalent scholarship on non-religious and personal grievance-based sources of jihadist radicalization, jihadization is rather explained as a process preceded by personal radicalization.[78]

Grievance.

The remaining two approaches examine the regional insurgency as essentially a homegrown phenomenon.[79] Rather than pointing to ideological factors or exogenous influences, the proponents of this approach have pointed to grievance as the principal cause of violent mobilization in the North Caucasus.[80] Grievance is a concept that has many meanings, and is applied differently by various scholars. Some authors examining the causes of the First Chechen War have pointed to grievance as drawing on the chosen trauma of the Stalin-era deportation of the Chechen people in 1944, which paved the way for a sense of shame and injustice shared by Chechens across generations. Once the regime relented and the self-declared Chechen state faced invasion by Russia, violent mobilization was facilitated by the collective sense of shame and injustice felt by the Chechens.[81] In a similar vein, Valery Tishkov, Brian Glyn Williams, and Aurélie Campana point to the grievance-centered concepts of collective memory and chosen trauma to explain the ease of the Chechens' violent mobilization on the eve of, and during the course of, the First Chechen War.[82] Nevertheless, as Cristoph Zürcher has observed in relation to other North Caucasian ethnic groups that were also deported but chose not to rebel (Karachay-Balkars and Ingush), chosen trauma and collective memory alone barely account for violent mobilization.[83] According to this line of reasoning, it is not ethnicity that generates conflict, but conflict that leads to the "ethnification" of identity. The latter includes the (re)construction of ethno-nationalist narratives centered on past grievances and injustices, with the "ethnic enemy" regarded as the source of such suffering. Against this background, the antithesis of grievance is greed, which may be defined as the motivation to acquire material benefits. Greed appears to be a rather minor cause of violent mobilization due to the absence of coveted resources in much of the North Caucasus.[84]

Seen from a different perspective, the grievance-centered approach posits that the brutality and impunity of federal and local security personnel, specifically military and police forces, have radicalized masses of North Caucasians. On the pretext of the "war against terrorism," local *siloviki* have conducted extrajudicial targeting of pious Muslims—who they have singled out as the insurgents' alleged sympathizers—as well as randomly selected youth. In addition, local police officers have sought to profit from counterterrorist campaigns. For example, imprisoning and torturing individuals in order to obtain confessions about their involvement in terrorist activity has enabled local police to refine their statistics, accelerate their careers, and receive funding from the federal budget on the pretext of successfully combating terrorism.[85] Other security officials (the *siloviki*) have resorted to kidnapping, and then demanding ransom money for their release.[86]

Russian and foreign human rights organizations have routinely reported on the excessive use of brutal interrogation techniques, abuse, and torture.[87] According to an estimate by Sapiyat Magomedova, a prominent Dagestani lawyer and human rights activist, only around 10 percent of all Dagestani "terrorists" or their supporters are incarcerated on substantiated grounds.[88] Indeed, the largely indiscriminate violence employed by the local and federal *siloviki* since the early-2000s has antagonized a segment of the North Caucasian population, of which hundreds and possibly even thousands of individuals have later joined local Salafi-jihadist groups. This, in turn, has created a vicious cycle of retaliation and counter-retaliation, with intelligence and security officials carrying out retributive attacks on actual or alleged insurgents and their alleged sympathizers. In keeping with the general scholarship, indiscriminate violence is believed to be conducive to violent mobilization in the North Caucasus.

Supported by recent ethnographic research, the grievance-centered approach has incorporated a novel perspective based on the prevalence of semi-archaic social codes in the eastern North Caucasus.[89] Pioneered by the present author, Huseyn Aliyev, and Jean-François Ratelle, this grievance-centered approach is centered on the crucial role that blood revenge plays as an apolitical source of violent mobilization. Against the background of the surviving code of retaliation, the clan-based organization of local societies has often resulted in the mobilization of several individuals, rather than just one, to retaliate following an offense.[90] Within this novel school of thought, grievance is approached as a systematized sociocultural process guided by the honor-centered notions of offense, shame, and retaliation. With the custom of blood revenge still intact in Chechnya, Ingushetia, and, to an extent, also in Dagestan, many local men who suffered immense humiliation and injury at the hands of *siloviki* never reconciled with these offenses. Driven by the honor-centered custom of blood revenge, these men seek to retaliate against the offenders, sometimes disregarding the costs of such retaliation to themselves or their families.[91] Those knowledgeable of the identities of the offenders have often chosen to retaliate on their own without joining jihadist groups. Those who lack such knowledge or who are otherwise unable to exact revenge on their own have typically joined jihadist groups. As a rule, those with knowledge of the actual culprit of an offense have sought to disengage immediately following the act of retaliation. On the other hand, those who have joined jihadist groups have usually been subjected to strong Salafi-jihadist indoctrination and are unwilling or unable to leave.[92]

Social Injustice, Unpopular Elites, and the Erosion of Traditionalist Values.

The third approach focuses on the background causes of violent mobilization. Local elites, which are not elected but are appointed by the Kremlin, and thus are strictly pro-Moscow, are frequently unpopular with residents and as such, are often identified as a major point of contention.[93] Moscow-backed local authorities—infamous for their impunity, corruption, and incompetence—have particularly alienated local populations. Numerous studies have pointed to unpopular elites, corruption, and unemployment as a breeding ground of terrorism in the North Caucasus.[94] As Ronald Dannreuther and Luke March have observed, Moscow's granting to North Caucasian autonomous republics under local strongmen's autocratic rule for the sake of pacifying the region:

> comes with dangers of increasing corruption and poor governance . . . driving opposition underground and potentially reigniting terrorist campaigns beyond the region.[95]

Against the background of high unemployment, a generation of disenfranchised youth has emerged in the North Caucasus. Without a peaceful and secular opposition to the local pro-Moscow regimes and in the face of grim personal prospects, Salafi-jihadism has asserted itself in the North Caucasus as a salient anti-establishment ideology, as observed elsewhere in the Muslim world.[96] Importantly, the appeal of Salafi-jihadism has been strong among the educated and middle-class North Caucasians.[97]

In addition to the preceding discussion, Ratelle and the present author have pointed to the rejection of "spoiled morals" — such as: the "frivolous" behavior of local women, the disappearance of customary law-centered social practices, lack of respect toward the elderly, drug addiction, and homosexuality, among others — as an important cognitive opening for the Dagestani youth to mobilize.[98] Many individuals in socially conservative Dagestan and other parts of the North Caucasus have accused local elites of the ongoing decline of Dagestan's age-old patriarchal values, drawing on Islam and local tradition. This has sharpened a sense of social injustice among the local population; and while this notion rarely pushes individuals to violent mobilization, it nevertheless makes them more receptive to anti-establishment sentiments. Against this background, Salafi-jihadism appears to have successfully branded itself as the defender of traditionalist values among a segment of Dagestani youth.[99]

SOURCES OF PRO-INSURGENT SUPPORT

Funding.

Against the impressive background of scholarship on the causes of violent mobilization in the North Caucasus, our knowledge is fragmented as to the sources of pro-insurgent support. In terms of funding, those in favor of viewing the North Caucasus insurgency as an imported phenomenon have tended to link it to outside sources of funding, particularly to al-Qaeda.

General consensus maintains that, while external organizations may have sponsored some jihadist groups since the early-2000s, particularly in Chechnya, this trend has faded away. Indeed, a number of observers have claimed that some Salafi-dominated charity organizations in the West and Middle East funneled funds to jihadist organizations, including those in the North Caucasus.[100]

Robert Schaefer has asserted that Chechnya-based pro-Salafi groups received funds directly from Saudi Arabia, Kuwait, Bahrain, and Qatar during the interwar period.[101] In a similar vein, Charlotte Hille has claimed that Chechen jihadists were financially aided by Saudi Arabia during the First Chechen War.[102] Chechen warlords themselves have lamented the lack of interest and financing from the outside, including other parts of the Muslim world. In a 2004 interview, Shamil Basayev asserted that he was "ashamed of the Muslims. During the three years since September 11, nobody at all has helped us."[103] Most have admitted that the onset of the Iraq War in 2003 brought about an abrupt end to the financing of Chechen jihadists from various Salafi funds and organizations. Reuven Paz, director of the Project for the Research of Islamist Movements (PRISM), summarized this perspective through his assertion that:

> the main turning point was in 2003 with the start of the Iraqi Jihadi insurgency. The focus on Iraq as an alternative arena for Afghanistan, caused al-Qaeda to lose interest in the Chechen struggle, and in Russia as a significant target. . . . Chechnya had become marginal in al-Qaeda's strategy.[104]

Today, only the staunchest proponents of the Chechen and North Caucasian insurgencies being an offspring of the global jihadist movement have claimed that they continue to receive money from the Middle East. In 2015, when reflecting on Russia's deteriorating relations with the United States, Putin even went so far as to claim that Chechen insurgents in the early-2000s received support from the United States.[105] Such allegations generally lack solid ground, such as Hahn's recent assertion that al-Qaeda finances the CE.[106] Hahn has pointed to two incidents to support his claim, the first of which was the May 2011 arrest in Prague by Czech police of eight North Caucasians suspected of plotting attacks in the North Caucasus. The second incident occurred when a statement of support by Abu Muhammad al-Maqdisi—a prominent Salafi-jihadist author of Jordanian-Palestinian origin, also known as Essam Muhammad Tahir al-Barqawi—was uploaded onto the North Caucasus insurgency websites. Hahn posited that such statements were proof of al-Qaeda's support for the North Caucasian jihadists, because the websites on which these statements were posted are used to raise money.

Statements of mutual support made by jihadists from various parts of the world are a routine practice often used to boost a sense of solidarity without entailing actual support. According to Hahn, the Czech police accused the arrested individuals of securing external financing for the North Caucasian jihadists, as reported by the Russian English-language news portal *Life.ru*. This information was soon negated by Robert Šlachta, head of the Czech special police force that carried out the arrest. According to Šlachta, the arrested individuals supposedly procured false IDs, weapons, and explosives for North Caucasian jihadists; however, no ties between the arrested individuals and al-Qaeda or external funding were discovered.[107]

Codes of Hospitality and Silence.

Recent ethnographic studies have supported the dominant perspective that the North Caucasian jihadists are cut off from external funding. In order to survive, individual jihadist groups must acquire funding on their own. Largely confined to mountainous passes, Chechen jihadists are extremely limited in terms of their contacts with the outside world. They usually rely on several hundred supporters — driven by either the local code of hospitality or by sympathies toward the insurgents — to provide supplies of food, warm clothes, medicine, weapons, and ammunition.[108]

In contrast to Dagestani jihadists, Chechens exercise no control on the ground. With increased incumbent control and with the insurgents' supporters subjected to harsh reprisals, the insurgents are unable to visit cities, go shopping, spend money, or perform other routine tasks.[109] In Dagestan, with its predominantly urban guerilla warfare, the insurgents' situation is easier than in Chechnya. While Chechen insurgents rely on a shrinking network of local supporters to obtain their basic needs, Dagestani local jihadi groups have rather diversified sources of financing. The present author and Akhmet Yarlykapov have shown that *zakat* — or the "money for jihad" — that is gathered both voluntarily and involuntarily provide Dagestani jihadists with a principal source of income. Storeowners are blackmailed into regularly paying money or face destruction of their businesses or death. Jihadists occasionally kidnap individuals and request ransom money to release them, or otherwise engage in economic criminal activities.[110]

Salafi-sympathizers both within and outside Dagestan also provide funding to local jihadi groups. According to a recent survey, 20 percent of Dagestani youth self-identify as "moderate" Salafis.[111] The actual number of Salafi-jihadists is not known, but they may form an important minority within Dagestan's Salafi community. Indiscriminate violence deployed by local *siloviki* against Salafis may push some of them to provide more tangible support to jihadists, apart from violent mobilization.[112]

An important source of pro-insurgent support, unrelated to theological convictions and political stances, is identified in recent work by the present author and Aliyev. The persistence of the sociocultural codes of hospitality and silence prompts some of the local population to provide support to the insurgents and to avoid collaboration with the authorities. In fact, these two codes, part of the customary law (*adat*) of the North Caucasian people, are enshrined in the regional tradition. The code of silence dictates that highlanders avoid collaboration with the authorities, including police, even if they themselves are in conflict with the local insurgents. In order not to "lose face" in the eyes of fellow villagers, locals are expected to provide support to insurgents as insiders—a custom that is prevalent particularly in socially conservative rural areas. In theory, support is to be provided regardless of reprisals or the political and religious views held by the locals. In the face of increasing reprisals by the authorities, it is difficult for the locals to find the motivation to provide such support. Nevertheless, this honor-bound support still constitutes an important source of pro-insurgent support that is difficult to trace and penalize.[113]

THE NORTH CAUCASIAN INSURGENCY

Organization.

While the Chechen insurgency experienced a sharp transition from ethno-nationalist separatism to a jihadist movement in the 2000s,[114] the insurgency in the rest of the North Caucasus has been dominated by Salafi-jihadist rhetoric from its very onset. With the exception of a segment of individual avengers who seek to retaliate on their own, and thereby avoid joining insurgent groups, the North Caucasus insurgency is overwhelmingly jihadi and consists of dozens of autonomous groups, numbering from five to 12 active members each. These jihadist groups are formally subordinated to a *vilayat* — or province — of which there are currently four: the *vilayats* of Nokhchichö or Chechnya, of Galgaychö or Ingushetia, of Dagestan, and of Kabarda-Balkaria-Karachay.[115] These *vilayats* are governed by *naibs* (governors; *amir's* deputies), who are formally appointed by the *amir* of the CE. Although *naibs* swear loyalty to the *amir*, the *amir's* control on the ground is, in reality, very limited.[116]

Across the North Caucasus, the term *jamaat* is used to designate local jihadi groups. In practice, subordination of one jihadi group to another is quite formal. Like jihadi groups operating in other parts of the world, the CE can be viewed as a brand or a franchise representing a horizontal network of loosely organized jihadi groups. *Jamaats* are highly autonomous and are ruled by individual leaders, or *amirs,* and operate in distinct areas or sectors for which they are responsible.[117] These jihadist groups are self-sufficient in terms of their recruitment and funding,[118] and they operate in isolation of each other, which on the one hand, reduces their overall effectiveness, and on the other hand, reduces the risk of being discovered, infiltrated, and liquidated. In spite of their relative isolation, these jihadi groups are bound together by their common ideology of Salafi-jihadism.[119]

Violence.

In the past, North Caucasian insurgencies occurred episodically in controlled small pockets of land. Due to increasingly fierce counterinsurgency operations and the incumbent's control on the ground, *jamaats* have been forced, however, to change their modes of organization and operation. Having become more loosely organized, jihadist groups mainly target security personnel—both federal and local—and local authorities within the region, as well as civilian targets outside the region in Russia proper. This phenomenon can be explained by the jihadists' efforts not to alienate local populations, who serve as current and potential supporters. In fact, civilians who have been killed as a result of insurgent attacks have mostly been bystanders and not the direct target of the attack itself.[120]

Jihadists have increasingly resorted to improvised explosive devices and bombing of infrastructure and mass transportation—particularly trains, subway stations, and airports.[121] Pro-regime clergy are sometimes attacked by these groups, with the assassination in Dagestan of the reputed Sufi sheikh Said Afandi Chirkeisky in August 2012 being perhaps the most well-known example. Since 2010, insurgents have periodically attacked casinos, liquor stores, and brothels—accusing them of being sources of sin. Insurgents nevertheless have usually sought to avoid killing local people during such attacks.[122] Suicide attacks have also been used, and are viewed as the jihadists' most feared and lethal method. The bombings in the Moscow subway stations and international airport during 2010–2011 claimed the lives of dozens of civilians.

Urban vs. Rural Guerillas.

Since 2007, most insurgent activity has been confined to the main urban areas and some mountainous areas of Dagestan, a number of mountainous areas of Chechnya and Ingushetia, and to some urban areas of Kabardino-Balkaria.[123] In Dagestan, the ongoing guerilla warfare is predominantly urban in terms of the intensity of insurgent violence. Makhachkala, Kizlyar, and Khasavyurt have been among the most frequented targets of insurgent violence in the Caspian republic. Rural areas, particularly those to the east of the capital city and in central Dagestan, have rather been used by insurgent groups as a safe haven—a situation that is being changed due to the incumbent forces' recent consolidated thrust into these areas. Since the early-2010s, the cities of southern Dagestan, followed by some wooded mountainous areas, have also been hit by insurgent violence. In Ingushetia and Dagestan, the borderland areas have witnessed the most violence, although insurgent groups have attacked other areas as well. The flatlands of northern Chechnya and the area to the north of the Terek River have, however, been spared of the conflict. In Kabardino-Balkaria, the capital city of Nalchik, along with some neighboring towns, has dominated the landscape of the local insurgency, although insurgent groups have also frequently attacked targets in the heavily mountainous south, as well as some central and northern areas of the republic.[124] In recent years, Dagestan has been the leader of the regional insurgency, followed by Chechnya and Ingushetia, with Kabardino-Balkaria the republic being least affected by conflict.

II. CHECHNYA 2000–2010: A MODEL COUNTERINSURGENCY?

SELECTIVE TARGETING

By the early-2000s, the Russian army had largely failed to annihilate the Chechen insurgency. On the one hand, the Russian army had broken the backbone of the Chechen resistance in the fierce fighting in and around Grozny at the end of 1999 and beginning of 2000, during which time hundreds of Chechen insurgents perished along with many gifted military commanders.[125] By that time, the Russian army had also gained control on the ground, at least during the day. Although Chechen insurgent groups were capable of dealing sensitive blows to the Russian military across the republic, Chechen insurgents were largely based in the wooded mountainous areas of central and southern Chechnya, and endured harsh winters, scarce food, and little contact with the outside world. On the other hand, the Russian military continued to struggle to localize and destroy the remaining insurgent groups. A Russian combat general reported from Chechnya, as late as 2004, that the federal troops were "so busy just trying to ensure their own security that they almost never can counter the resurgent guerrillas."[126]

The principal cause of the Russian military's failure was its excessive use of indiscriminate violence, which resulted from its lack of information about the insurgents and their social networks. Instead of reducing insurgent violence, it multiplied it, as masses of aggrieved Chechens—even those with no prior wish to do so—sought to join insurgent groups in order to retaliate.

It was the gradual deployment of the *kadyrovtsy* in combat as part of Moscow's Chechenization strategy that changed the course of the protracted war. There were various reasons for Chechens to join the paramilitary units subordinated directly to the Kadyrov family—Moscow's main proxy in the troublesome republic.[127] Having made enemies among the jihadist-dominated insurgency in previous years, some former fighters—who were predominantly nationalist-minded—sought to defect to the pro-Russian side in order to settle a score with their enemies and their families. Others joined the *kadyrovtsy* units because of pressure put on them by Russian authorities and their Chechen proxies. In fact, in the early-2000s, relatives of renowned Chechen insurgent commanders were hijacked *en masse*. The commanders were forced to either capitulate, defect, or face the killing of their relatives.[128] Many (predominantly non-Salafi-minded) commanders eventually sought to defect in order to save the lives of their loved ones, and they usually brought their foot soldiers, fellow clan members, or neighbors with them. Others joined either the *kadyrovtsy* or Chechnya's newly formed pro-Moscow government institutions because they had been promised high-ranking positions and security by Akhmad Kadyrov, the head of the pro-Moscow Chechen government whom they had known previously. In addition to experienced veterans, Chechen youth also joined the *kadyrovtsy* as they sought to obtain security for themselves and members of their families against the background of increasingly intense and largely indiscriminate violence perpetrated by Russian troops.[129] Once deployed in combat against insurgents or in raids against the insurgents' relatives, these new recruits became "bound by blood" to the Kadyrov family. As the killing of an insurgent or his relative by a pro-Moscow Chechen paramilitary troop initiated a blood feud among the families involved, the *kadyrovtsy* had no way out but to remain committed to their new leader, whatever the recruits' prior political convictions.[130]

The deployment of the *kadyrovtsy* from among former insurgents was crucial for a number of reasons. First, having direct knowledge of the insurgents' modes of organization and operation — including their identities, mountainous hideouts, and networks — the former insurgents in the ranks of the *kadyrovtsy* paramilitaries were able to deploy selective violence against their former comrades-in-arms. Familiar with the insurgents' local social networks, the *kadyrovtsy* were much more effective in tracing the sources of pro-insurgent support among the local population than the Russian troops were. As a result, mop-up operations — known as *zachistkas* — carried out by the *kadyrovtsy* have been much more effective than those carried out by Russian troops. Supported by Russian troops as a backup force, the *kadyrovtsy* conducted forced disappearances of the insurgents' supporters and relatives.[131] In fact, in order to increase control on the ground, Russian military garrisons were established near Chechen villages that were considered to be critical in terms of insurgent violence and where the *kadyrovtsy* had also established permanent bases.[132] In some areas, *zachistkas* became a continuous phenomenon together with routine forced disappearances.[133] As a result, during the peak of the *kadyrovtsy*-led raids and *zachistkas* of the mid-2000s, the leading Russian human rights organization, Memorial, reported the discovery of around 50 mass graves containing the bodies of hundreds of Chechens, most of them with traces of severe injuries and bodily mutilation.[134] During the period 1999–2004, Memorial recorded 2,090 cases of such forced disappearances, which were attributed to both the Russian army and the *kadyrovtsy*.[135] Over the years, the *kadyrovtsy* have become a much-feared force in Chechnya, which — in contrast to Russian troops — have usually applied selective violence by directly targeting insurgents and their supporters. Greater knowledge and understanding of the insurgents and their whereabouts also facilitated the deployment of artillery, helicopters, and armored vehicles much more effectively than before. Over time, this has contributed to the dramatic decline of insurgent activity in Chechnya.

Due to the isolation of the remaining groups of Chechen insurgents in heavily mountainous areas, they have evolved to have no financial requirements in order to operate. These Chechen insurgents' contacts with the outside world have become confined to several hundred supporters who help the insurgents meet their basic needs. With rare exceptions, these insurgents are no longer able to travel to villages and cities to spend their money. This was still possible in the 2000s, however, when incumbent control on the ground was not well established. To curb the sources of insurgent funding, Chechnya's pro-Moscow government increased control over Chechen diaspora communities in Chechnya, Russian cities, and Europe — an important source of funding for Chechen insurgents.[136]

Chechen authorities have cooperated with Russian intelligence services and Russia's diplomatic representations in European countries, going so far as to establish Chechen departments in a number of Russian embassies, with the aim of infiltrating and controlling the work of local Chechen communities. According to some sources, Chechens funneling money to Chechnya-based insurgent groups through attachés were targeted in Europe and in the Middle East,[137] which gradually led to the reduction of support by Chechen community organizations, even those based outside of Russia. Concerned about their relatives in Chechnya being targeted in acts of retribution, many Chechens have sought to distance themselves from supporting Chechen insurgents back home or even expressing critical views of Chechnya's pro-Moscow government in general and the Kadyrov family in particular.[138]

COLLECTIVE PUNISHMENT

Since the early-2000s, Chechnya has largely found itself outside of Russia's legal space. Extrajudicial executions, torture, and abuse—including sexual abuse— have become widespread phenomena, engulfing the activities of both Russian troops and their Chechen allies.[139] Although the scale of human rights violations has lessened in recent years, many Chechens—aware of the increasingly high cost of pro-insurgent support and violent mobilization—have sought to stay away from insurgency and insurgency-related violence.

Since the early-2000s, and particularly in the mid-2000s, Chechen authorities have deployed the principle of collective punishment against insurgents' relatives. Individuals joining insurgent groups should have anticipated that their allegiance to such groups would scarcely go unnoticed and that their relatives would be held accountable for their membership. In the 2000s, the *kadyrovtsy* routinely killed the relatives of insurgents, with such killings taking the form of forced disappearances described in detail in the previous section of this monograph. Having obtained information on the local youth who had allegedly joined an insurgent group, armored vehicles carrying masked *kadyrovtsy* — often aided by Russian troops — would enter a village and then kidnap the youth's relative or relatives. The authorities would usually refuse to communicate with the abducted man's relatives and would threaten to capture another male from the same family if the captured individual chose to complain. With the *kadyrovtsy* enjoying impunity in Chechen and federal courts, most Chechen families chose to remain silent on the matter. The abducted individual would either disappear without a trace or be found later in either a personal or a mass grave, with the authorities labeling it as the liquidation of an insurgent.

Aware of the uproar it could cause, Grozny has been careful never to openly endorse or confirm the tactical application of the principle of collective guilt. The pro-Moscow Chechen authorities on multiple occasions have publicly stated that some form of co-responsibility was indispensable for the relatives of insurgents. They have, however, usually avoided being explicit about using lethal violence against insurgents' relatives. For example, Ramzan Kadyrov asserted in a 2009 interview that it was justifiable for the incumbent forces to use the relatives of insurgents as human shields during counterinsurgency operations.[140] In a 2010 speech, Kadyrov issued an explicit warning to insurgents' relatives, stating that, "having allowed such filth to go to the woods [to join the insurgency], those fathers and brothers should know that we will hold them to accountable."[141] Kadyrov and his closest associates continued to make similar statements in subsequent years.[142]

Against the backdrop of intense reprisals, many Chechens have sought to either postpone retaliation—an important trigger of violent mobilization—or to abandon it outright in order not to expose their families to excessive violence. In a similar vein, many Chechens, supportive of the jihadists, have chosen to stay away from them in order to survive. Since the late-2000s and particularly since the 2010s, the decreasing support for insurgents and violent mobilization has led Chechen authorities to prefer non-lethal means of collective punishment—such as burning the houses of incriminated insurgents—over lethal means.[143] Reports nevertheless show that killings, particularly in the form of forced disappearances, are still executed by Chechnya's pro-Moscow authorities.[144]

Collective punishment of insurgents' relatives has proven to be an effective deterrent in Chechnya.[145] Concerned about the survival of their relatives, many insurgents have capitulated or defected, which in turn has led to the fragmentation of the insurgency from within. At the same time, some would-be insurgents have chosen to refrain from violent mobilization in general and joining *jamaats* in particular.[146] Ekaterina Sokirianskaya, the International Crisis Group's expert on the North Caucasus, has asserted that, "due to the horrible dictatorship [in Chechnya] and methods of collective punishment, the Chechens have postponed [the] blood feud and their protest to better times, which is impossible today. Still, this is a frozen situation, not a [sustainable] solution [to the conflict]."[147]

Even against the background of fierce reprisals, dozens of Chechens—driven by the code of honor—have sought to mobilize in order to avenge the wrongs inflicted upon themselves or their relatives by the *kadyrovtsy*.[148] Importantly, however, retaliation has been increasingly carried out by individual avengers on their own without joining insurgent groups, although a number of recruits have still sought to join these groups.[149] There are a number of possible explanations for this phenomenon: first, facing an intense manhunt, Chechen *jamaats* have become increasingly difficult to contact and approach. Second, unlike in previous years, *jamaats* have become largely incapable of providing prospective insurgents with weapons, ammunition, or the technical aid needed to exact revenge. Third, while many individual avengers have sought to target actual culprits of previous grievances, the Salafi-jihadist *jamaats* have gradually come to develop a novel and ideologically influenced agenda. The *jamaats'* understanding of their enemy and their targets is thus considerably broader than in the case of most individual avengers. Prospective avengers have therefore sought to retaliate on their own and, on some occasions, have used networks of relatives for retaliation. According to a Chechen political scientist, this explains Chechen insurgents' lack of prior knowledge of episodic, and often suicidal, attacks carried out by individual Chechens avengers.[150] A suicide bombing in downtown Grozny in October 2014 that claimed the lives of five *kadyrovtsy* is attributed to individual avengers.[151]

Although it has increased the cost of violent mobilization and pro-insurgent support, collective punishment has still not deterred hundreds of Chechens from providing support to local insurgent groups. In fact, at least 100 insurgents are believed to be currently hiding in Chechnya's mountains.[152] Confined to some densely wooded areas, these groups are isolated from the rest of the world due to the increasing ground control exercised by the *kadyrovtsy*. Given the conditions on the ground, this small but significant force would not be able to exist without local support. According to former insurgents, the local code of hospitality, together with personal or political sympathies, are what still motivate hundreds of locals to provide support to the Chechen insurgents, even in the face of daunting odds and risks.[153]

INFILTRATION AND DECAPITATION

During the 2000s, counterinsurgents made frequent use of infiltration and decapitation tactics in Chechnya as a means of destroying the insurgents' leadership and undermining the insurgent groups from within. Perhaps the most well-known case is the liquidation of Shamil Basayev by a Russian security service — *Federalnaya Sluzhba Bezopasnosti* (FSB) — agent in the Ingush village of Ekazhevo in July 2006. According to a Russian media outlet, having penetrated the jihadists' ranks:

> an FSB agent infiltrated Basayev's retinue and tipped off his superiors that Basayev had a KamAZ truck with three secret caches of explosives, arms and ammunition . . . An FSB agent was next to Basayev several hours before the blast and filmed him on his mobile phone camera, it said.[154]

It is likely that the agent was among those unnamed service members decorated by Putin for Basayev's killing the same year.[155] A similar assassination took place in March 2002, when a Dagestani agent hired by the FSB gained the trust of *amir* Khattab, an infamous Saudi-born jihadist, and the most well-known "Arab Afghan" in Chechnya. Serving as a messenger from Khattab's Saudi Arabia-based mother and Khattab himself, he gave the jihadist leader a poisoned letter that was coated with "a fast-acting nerve agent, possibly sarin or a derivative."[156] Similarly, a group of intelligence service agents entered and disrupted the group of another infamous Chechen jihadist, Salman Raduyev, in March 2000.[157] According to Anna Politkovskaya, the late reputed journalist who reported for the liberal Russian daily newspaper *Novaya Gazeta*, Khanpasha Terkipayev — a Chechen mole in the service of the Russian intelligence service — infiltrated the Chechen commando that seized the building of the Dubrovka theater in October 2002.[158]

Cognizant of the support provided by some of the local population to the insurgents, Russian intelligence service agents, aided by the *kadyrovtsy*, forced Chechen villagers to supply insurgents with poisoned food.[159] On some occasions, agents camouflaged as local villagers were used for this task. According to an FSB officer, in 2010 alone, more than 17 insurgents lost their lives due to poisoned food provided by locals.[160] Important jihadist leaders such as: Yasir Amat, Magarbi Temiraliyev, and Abubakar Pashayev, as well as their fellow fighters, were killed by consuming poisoned food, or suffered grave injuries from which they never recovered. Even the then-leader of the CE, Dokka Umarov, suffered greatly from injuries caused by poisoned food, having acquired a number of serious diseases that most likely led to his death in 2013. According to an FSB officer, as "tracing down and destroying fighters in the mountains is extremely difficult," operations involving poisoned food and drawing on the local population's code of hospitality-centered support, have continued, and have become increasingly widespread since 2009.[161]

The decapitation of Chechen insurgent leadership failed to lead to their ultimate decline, as elsewhere in the world. This infiltration, particularly the liquidation of dozens of Chechen fighters, including several gifted veterans and commanders, has nevertheless inflicted a heavy toll on them. While first-hand data on the impact of infiltration and decapitation tactics on the organization and operation of affected Chechen *jamaats* is lacking, the overall decline in insurgent activity in the sectors previously hit by infiltrations and decapitations speaks to the debilitation and paralysis of the *jamaats*.

III. COUNTERINSURGENCY

SELECTIVE TARGETING

As early as 2012, the Russian authorities were utilizing a number of tactical innovations, particularly in Dagestan, as the crucial epicenter of the regional insurgency, to facilitate the deployment of selective violence — meaning violence aimed against the insurgents and their supporters. Most importantly, elite counterinsurgency forces have been increasingly deployed in combat across the North Caucasus.[162] For example, the Special Rapid Response Units (SOBR) of the Russian Ministry of the Interior have featured prominently in the counterterrorist and counterinsurgent operations conducted in the North Caucasus, and particularly in Dagestan. On the republican level, the Special Purpose Mobility Units (OMON) falling under the jurisdiction of the local branches of the Ministry of Interior have been expanded since 2010 to take on the task of combating jihadists.[163] Counterinsurgency forces have also been aided by the FSB, which has turned the North Caucasus into its principal site of work.[164]

The need to deploy elite counterinsurgency units became apparent on the eve of the Winter Olympic Games in the southern city of Sochi, situated in the Kranosdar Province just hundreds of miles away from the battlefield. Over the previous decade, most fighting was done by the various detachments of the republican branches of the Ministry of Interior, specializing in counterterrorism, and the local police.[165] Known for their incompetence, corruption, and nepotism, the republican police have proved to be poor counterinsurgents, but brutal torturers.[166] For example, Dagestani police have collaborated on various occasions with the insurgents over economic issues, such as control over local businesses.[167] There is evidence of some Dagestani *jamaats* having morphed into organized crime groups with excessive ties to district and even republican authorities — including police officers, who are usually intertwined with civil authorities.[168] Due to the salience of kinship ties in North Caucasian society, local police have on various occasions warned, and even refused to attack, their relatives in the ranks of jihadist groups of forthcoming operations.[169] In Dagestan, where unemployment among youth has been particularly high, many have sought to join the police by bribing the authorities.[170] When admitted, police officers have sought to regain, and even multiply, their investment instead of risking their lives in combat. They have thus been involved in abductions, racketeering, and the targeting of alleged jihadists and their supporters for the sake of improving their record. In addition, some police officers have also been largely unwilling to engage in violent encounters with the insurgents, preferring less violent and more beneficial activities instead. Some local police units also lack proper training to fight insurgents.[171]

The deployment of elite counterinsurgency forces has partially replaced local police units and has helped solve a number of problems. Being properly trained and lacking local attachments, these elite units have proven to be a much-more-effective counterinsurgency force than local police units.[172] Unlike local police, elite counterinsurgency forces in the North Caucasus have proven to be highly determined and unhindered by the corruption and nepotism plaguing local police units, with counterinsurgency operations being kept secret from the local authorities until the very last moment; that has proven to be a major issue, particularly in Dagestan's rural areas with highly developed kinship ties.[173] In a similar vein, counterinsurgency operations conducted by elite forces have been on the offensive in Kabardino-Balkaria and Ingushetia.[174]

Importantly, Russian authorities have focused on breaking the insurgents' support base, with Ivan Sydoruk acknowledging that federal and local *siloviki* have increasingly targeted those who provide insurgents with various forms of support.[175] In contrast to previous years, insurgents' supporters have been killed without trial in a series of recent insurgent operations.[176] In addition, artillery shelling has frequently been used to destroy the homes of insurgents' supporters during special operations.[177] Since 2012, *zachistkas* have increasingly been carried out in Dagestan, and they have hit not only urban centers, but also mountainous areas with little or no previous control by the authorities.[178] Importantly, *zachistkas* carried out by elite counterinsurgency forces, made up of both federal and republican troops, have been reminiscent of the *kadyrovtsy's* mode of operation. Unlike the Russian troops that resorted to indiscriminate violence in the early-2000s, *zachistkas* conducted by elite forces have drawn on information gathered from intelligence and have therefore been much more selective.

Having learned lessons from the Chechen campaigns, mop-up operations have also been, on the whole, more focused and less lethal than in Chechnya. Although human rights organizations and journalists have decried the destruction of property and looting that often accompanied the mop-up operations in Dagestan,[179] civilians unrelated to the insurgents or their supporters are usually evacuated from the affected villages. As a rule, *zachistkas* are not accompanied by large-scale violence, even though—as this section will later demonstrate—the practice of forced disappearances has still been used.

Zachistkas, which in many ways have become a continuous presence, have led to the decline in the scale of insurgent violence in the affected areas since the end of 2012 and the beginning of 2013. There are two main reasons for this decline: (1) the permanent deployment of elite counterinsurgency forces backed by armored regiments of the Russian army (see below) in the vicinity of insurgent hotbeds;[180] and, (2) the protracted mop-ups that have disrupted insurgent group's social networks in their areas of operation, resulting in a considerable decrease in supplies of food, clothes, and ammunition from the local population.[181]

Another innovation used by the incumbent has been the simultaneous deployment, since late-2012, of the Russian army units in Dagestan.[182] In this regard, the Russian army once again appears to have learned lessons from its previous involvement in Chechnya. Instead of carrying out mop-ups, Russian troops have rather provided backup for elite counterinsurgency forces in such operations conducted by the latter. The Russian troops have sought to isolate the rural mountainous areas from the main urban centers with the aim of separating urban-based insurgent groups from their mountainous hideouts. This aims to disable insurgents in urban areas who are under pressure to escape to their at one time rarely disturbed safe havens in the mountainous areas of central Dagestan. Communication between rural and urban *jamaats* has also been disrupted and, with the insurgents' safe havens coming under increasing fire, their flexibility has been significantly reduced.[183]

COLLECTIVE PUNISHMENT

In previous years, attempts to initiate the practice of collective punishment—likely initiated by Moscow—took place in the North Caucasus, but eventually failed to gain momentum on the regional level. In Kabardino-Balkaria, for example, a group calling itself the Black Hawks (*Chernie yastreby*) was formed in 2011. The members of the group issued several videos in which they, with their faces covered by masks, called for the Chechnya-style retributive liquidation of insurgents' relatives to be a legitimate means of fighting the local insurgency.[184] The activists hinted at the revival of the custom of blood feud, which was no longer being practiced in that part of the Caucasus. At the time, many commentators considered this to be an FSB-led attempt to intimidate members of the local insurgency.[185] This initiative eventually faded away, possibly because the local population rejected it based on their belief that retributive violence against innocent people is an illegitimate form of combat.

Similar calls have episodically been made by some politicians and intellectuals in Dagestan, but to no avail thus far. An incident in the village of Khajalmakhi in Dagestan's Levashi District nevertheless constitutes a special exception. In early-2013, an "execution list," containing the names of 33 local inhabitants—some of them Salafis—allegedly sympathizing with or providing support to the local jihadists was produced. In March, three people from the list were killed under questionable circumstances, and an additional four people from the blacklist were later assassinated. Local and republican police largely distanced themselves from the incidents, demonstrating their inability or unwillingness to investigate the cases.

Despite the huge impacts of the killings on Dagestani society, no one was charged, and the killer(s) continue to circumvent justice to this day. With the local police refusing to interfere in village affairs, some of which even claimed that they had no knowledge of the existence of this "execution list," most families associated with Salafis, jihadists, or their sympathizers soon chose to leave the village.[186] Similar initiatives have also emerged on the federal level in recent years. Members of the State Duma, the lower house of Russia's parliament, unequivocally passed a bill requiring terrorists' relatives to pay for damages caused by attacks in late-2013.[187]

Collective punishment targeting insurgents' relatives has increasingly been used by Russian and local authorities in the North Caucasus beyond Chechnya's borders. While it has been mostly non-lethal in Kabardino-Balkaria and Ingushetia, collective punishment has become an increasingly lethal practice in Dagestan, where *zachistkas* have been on the rise. Although journalists and representatives of human rights organizations have been routinely barred from entering villages subjected to mop-up operations, recent reports indicate that counterinsurgency forces have adopted the Chechen practice of destroying the homes of relatives of Dagestani insurgents. Human Rights Watch, for example, reported on the mop-up of Gimry—a stronghold of the Dagestani insurgency—by OMON in 2014, along with other villages, and pointed to "bombed-out" houses and individuals that disappeared by force over the course of often protracted *zachistkas*.[188] According to a statement by the press service of the Dagestani President, in August 2013 alone, 10 houses were destroyed during mop-ups in the republic.[189] The homes of insurgents' relatives have been blown up across Dagestan, including in Buynaksk, Sasitli, and even in the republic's capital city, Makhachkala.[190]

Most alarmingly, the feared practice of forced disappearances, previously applied in Chechnya, have been introduced in Dagestan, with abducted individuals disappearing without a trace. In September 2014 alone, 19 men from the village of Vremenniy disappeared by force during a local mop-up, with the whereabouts of most of them remaining unknown.[191] The total number of individuals who have disappeared by force is difficult to establish, but estimates suggest that up to 100 individuals, predominantly young males, have been abducted thus far, most of them disappearing without a trace.[192] According to *Novaya Gazeta*, Dagestani authorities have adopted a new policy of firing insurgents' relatives in the ranks of police and local authorities as a new counterinsurgency tactic.[193]

INFILTRATION AND DECAPITATION

In the late-2000s, North Caucasian *jamaats* saw their numbers of recruits skyrocket. Determined either to retaliate against wrongs inflicted upon them by police or to challenge the corrupt and "spoiled" regime, hundreds of young Dagestanis, Ingush, Kabardins, and Balkarians joined locally operating insurgent groups. Once fairly small and isolated groups of fighters with individual knowledge of each other that often dated back to pre-war times, *jamaats* soon grew into relatively large groups. With dozens of members each, this once-valued personalized knowledge became a rare commodity among the ranks of jihadists, particularly in Dagestan—where recruitment was particularly high. During that period, insurgency became so popular among the local population that it included the sons or relatives of high-ranking members of republican elites, as well as reputed athletes, former government officials, and highly educated individuals with Ph.D. degrees.[194] The rise of members of insurgent groups during that period significantly contributed to the peak of insurgent attacks observed during 2010–2013.

On the other hand, recruitment of this magnitude soon pointed to the weakness of the insurgent groups, which had been increasingly infiltrated by agents and moles.[195] A number of recent crackdowns on jihadist groups are indicative of this shift.[196] With agents planted by *siloviki* in the ranks of rebel groups, infiltrated *jamaats* saw their hideouts revealed, fellow jihadists and their supporters targeted, and dozens of insurgents lose their lives.[197]

Hand in hand with the ongoing infiltration of jihadist groups, authorities have also sought to target the leadership of *jamaats*. In Chechnya, one such prominent infiltration that led to decapitation took place in early-2013.[198] At the time, the installation of a 21-year old mole, Islam Temishev, into the group led by the prominent and skilled veteran leaders Husayn and Muslim Gakayevs—who are considered as Ramzan Kadyrov's personal enemies—resulted in the death of 12 Chechen fighters, including the rebel brothers. The killing of the Gakayev brothers was followed by a period of relative calm as jihadists needed to regroup and select new leadership.[199] The liquidation in early-2014 of Tengiz Guketlov in Kabardino-Balkaria, and Artur Gatagazhev in Ingushetia, also brought about a lull in insurgent activity. The killing in April 2015 of the formal *amir* of the CE, Aliaskhab Kebekov in his hideout,

as well as the recent killings of a number of Dagestani jihadist commanders, have also been attributed to
authorities' implantation of moles in locally operating
jihadist groups from late-2009 to 2013.[200]

As in Chechnya, the infiltration of insurgent
groups and their decapitation have led to the considerable weakening of the targeted groups. First-hand
data, notoriously difficult to obtain, is lacking for targeted insurgent groups in the North Caucasus. Available figures, however, point to an abrupt decline in
insurgent activity in those areas over which targeted
jamaats had claimed responsibility. This could be the
main cause behind the recent absence of news on insurgent violence in the Kabardino-Balkaria's Nalchik
area, where Guketlov was killed; in Ingushetia, where
Gatagazhev was killed; and in Chechnya's southeast,
where the now-deceased Gakayev brothers were operating. As in the case of Chechnya, the decapitated
groups are likely to have been paralyzed and thus are
largely incapable of carrying out insurgent or terrorist
activity for the months to come.

THE RECRUITMENT OF NORTH CAUCASIANS
INTO THE SYRIAN CIVIL WAR

Faced with increasingly effective counterinsurgency operations and decreasing local support, the
leadership of local insurgent groups has had to confront yet another challenge: the growing appeal of the
Islamic State to local youth. Jihadist groups' internal
squabbles,[201] collaboration with the authorities, and
clandestine lives lived permanently on the run have
alienated frustrated youth from local jihadist groups.
Some of these youth have been outraged by the Syrian
regime's inhumane treatment of their Sunni Muslim

brethren. According to a former Dagestani jihadist speaking about the death of a slain fellow jihadist, "[h]e went to Syria because he couldn't stand that Assad and his army were killing children."[202] Others were inspired by the spectacular advances of the Islamic State, which currently controls large swathes of land. As a result, hundreds of Dagestanis and other North Caucasians have traveled to the Middle East to partake in the local armed conflict. While many appear to have been fascinated by the revolutionary appeal of Salafi-jihadism, others have sought to travel to Syria to help their fellow believers.[203]

According to a recent statement by Alexander Bortnikov, head of the FSB, as many as 2,000 Russian citizens, most of them presumably of North Caucasian origin, may have been involved in the Syrian Civil War.[204] Importantly, Russian intelligence services have done little to prevent North Caucasian youth from traveling to Turkey and then on to Syria.[205] Some commentators have speculated that this is due to Moscow's motivation to dispose of the disenfranchised and frustrated local youth in order to weaken the North Caucasus insurgency.[206] Indeed, over the course of the past 2 years or so, hundreds of prospective recruits who would have joined local insurgent groups have chosen to travel to Syria, which has weakened local *jamaats*. This has presented local *jamaats* with a previously unprecedented short supply of new recruits.[207]

As the exodus of frustrated North Caucasians traveling to Syria would weaken insurgent groups operating in the North Caucasus, Moscow's lack of concern over Russian citizens traveling to Syria is understandable. Some North Caucasian jihadists have expressed an interest in returning to their native region once the war in the Middle East is over; however, due to high casualty rates among jihadists fighting in Syria and Iraq, only some are likely to make it back to their home region. In the end, having married local women, and motivated by the quest to carry out a "holy war" elsewhere in the Muslim world, not all North Caucasians will eventually seek to return to Russia or be allowed to enter Russian territory.[208] It is likely that Russia's interests in the conflict in Syria are at least partly related to its desire to have North Caucasian jihadists perish far away from their home region.[209]

The Syrian Civil War, and North Caucasian volunteers' willingness to participate in it, is an exogenous factor over which the Russian authorities have had a limited influence. Even so, Russian authorities have made effective use of the Syrian jihad to divert recruits away from the North Caucasus insurgency.

LIMITATIONS

Selective Targeting.

The massive deployment of elite counterinsurgency units since 2013 has been instrumental in breaking the backbone of many insurgent groups, and these units' ability to apply violence selectively has been crucial to this task. In fact, indiscriminate violence widely used by local police units has resulted in thousands of frustrated individuals across the North Caucasus, many of whom have sought to either retaliate or support insurgents. On the other hand, selective violence has been deployed in a more focused way by targeting insurgents and their supporters, with non-combatants largely left unharmed.

The deployment of elite counterinsurgency forces in combat, however, has not been without its limits.

The first of these limits is that these forces have been numerically weak. In Dagestan, for example, despite efforts to expand the local OMON units, they still number only a few hundred. This is caused partly by the locals' lack of willingness to join these units, and partly by strict screening procedures.[210] Today, OMON has around 20,000 members throughout Russia, with federal OMON — or OMON stemming from Russia proper — having been deployed in Dagestan or elsewhere in the North Caucasus only episodically. Due to the outsiders' lack of proper knowledge of the regional social landscape, North Caucasian OMON troops are usually preferred over non-local ones.[211] Functioning essentially as a riot police force, the various detachments of OMON consist of members that are sufficiently better trained, equipped, and in general more physically and psychologically fit than their counterparts in ordinary police units. While OMON units are trained to carry out *zachistkas* in local villages and towns,[212] their ability to combat insurgents on the ground is rather limited. In addition, OMON is widely used in other parts of Russia, constituting the regime's major force against the feared threat of popular "color revolutions" (the name stemming from the popular rebellions in Ukraine and Georgia, called the Orange and Rose Revolutions respectively).

A cross between riot police and a paramilitary force, SOBR units are trained specifically to be deployed in Special Weapons and Tactics (SWAT)-type special operations in direct combat with actual insurgents. As the Russian SOBR has only around 5,000 members scattered among Russia's major cities,[213] only a limited number of SOBR units may be simultaneously deployed in Dagestan or other parts of the North Caucasus.[214] Despite having a large ground force numbering slightly less than 800,000 troops, and a police force of more than 900,000 service members, the number of elite armed forces in Russia is notoriously low.

The current draining of local *jamaats*, partly caused by the outflow of many frustrated youth to Syria, has enabled these elite units to carry out concentrated attacks on insurgents and their supporters. Given recent developments, however, this situation may fundamentally change in the near future. For example, the flow of North Caucasian volunteers traveling to Syria may be reduced. Alternatively, Russia's hybrid war in eastern Ukraine—where such elite units have been deployed *en masse*—or in Syria, where Moscow has been increasingly aiding the al-Assad regime,[215] may divert them from the North Caucasus theater.[216] There is also evidence that Moscow has already redeployed some of these elite troops from the North Caucasus to the war in eastern Ukraine.[217] According to the news portal *Kavkazskaya politika* (Caucasian Politics):

> As of now the relocation of experienced servicemen from the regions of the North Caucasian Federal District to southeastern Ukraine has started and the relocated individuals are mainly not Caucasians. . . . This will significantly weaken Russian forces and undermine their work against the armed underground in the North Caucasus. No doubt, this will allow the militants of the Caucasus Emirate to strengthen their ranks at least to some extent, if not overpower the Russian forces.[218]

Against the background of Russia's dearth of elite troops, it cannot be completely ruled out that, should the circumstances necessitate, local police forces may once again become the main counterinsurgency force in the region. Even today, local police units have been deployed as an auxiliary counterinsurgency force during *zachistkas* or other raids. Local police units also continue to carry out preventive attacks, that are largely indiscriminate and incompetent, on insurgents' alleged supporters and sympathizers. In the face of elite forces' decreasing involvement in special operations outside of Russia, local police have returned to the forefront of regional counterinsurgency.[219] The authorities' inability to combat the persisting corruption and nepotism in the region, including within the security personnel, suggests that *siloviki* will not be an effective counterinsurgency force in the near future.

Having disrupted insurgents' ties with their supporters among the local population, *zachistkas* have led to an immediate decrease in insurgent activity in the affected areas. In the short term, *zachistkas* have proven to be effective in breaking the insurgents' networks of local supporters, as villagers must first take care of themselves and their families before providing support to insurgents. During *zachistkas*, villagers are usually evacuated away from their area to camps in open fields, even during cold months.[220] What appears to be a success in the short term, however, will not necessarily translate into permanent success. Following weeks or months of *zachistkas*, OMON units withdraw from the vicinity of "besieged" villages, and some of the local population — antagonized by the incumbent's behavior — seek to continue providing the remaining insurgents with support.[221] As the following writing demonstrates, while successful in the short term, *zachistkas* may generate masses of frustrated males sympathizing with the counterinsurgents, which in the end could cause the situation in the affected areas to deteriorate in subsequent years.

Additionally, the deployment of Russian army units in Dagestan has reportedly led to rivalry, miscommunication, and mutual animosity between the predominantly ethnic-Russian units of the Russian army and the local *siloviki*, comprised almost exclusively of members of indigenous ethnic groups. This has somewhat reduced the effectiveness of the military operations conducted in this North Caucasian republic, as collaboration between local police and the Russian "newcomers" has not been without issue. For example, local police have refrained from providing Russian counterinsurgents with accurate intelligence or have avoided subordination to ethnic Russian officers in charge of special operations.[222]

Information about the authorities' efforts to curb the financing of Dagestani, Ingush, and Kabardino-Balkar *jamaats* is scarce. From the information available, most experts assert that—in contrast to Kadyrov's fruitful initiatives to maintain his grip over the Chechen diaspora communities in Russia and Europe and their money transfers to Chechen insurgents—no such initiatives have been pushed forward by federal or Dagestani authorities.[223] This may be caused by the very multi-ethnic character of Dagestani diaspora communities. Dagestan's ethnic mosaic has resulted in the existence of a variety of power centers and ethnic multipolarity, as well as fluid ethnic or clan coalitions, all of which are difficult to control. Chechnya, a republic of more than 1 million inhabitants, has been ruled by a single, authoritarian, and mono-ethnic leadership that has imposed strict control over the local population, including control over the flow of money into the republic. It also forces the local population to pay tribute to the regime on a regular basis.[224] With nearly 3 million inhabitants, Dagestan, on the other hand, is a pluralistic society in which strict control over the republic's political and economic spheres, including its financial resources, is difficult to impose.

In addition, most of the funding for Dagestani (and Kabardino-Balkarian) *jamaats* appears to come from their "taxing" of local businesses. This is not the case in Chechnya, however, where businesses are forced to pay tribute directly to the Kadyrov family. To prevent these local businesses from being blackmailed and targeted by local jihadists, authorities have to provide these businesses, their owners, and employees with a substantial degree of personal safety. This, however, is a very demanding task, because providing personal protection to these individuals and their families goes well beyond the capabilities of the local police. This is also unlikely due to the widespread corruption of the republican police and administration. Underqualified and poorly paid, local police officers have shown immense interest in imposing their own "taxes" on local businesses, and protecting them is not on their agenda.

Collective Punishment.

While the incumbent has increasingly deployed lethal forms of collective punishment against insurgents' relatives in Dagestan, in Ingushetia and Kabardino-Balkaria — where insurgent violence has been decreasing — it has largely been spared. The scale of lethal violence being perpetrated against Dagestani insurgents' relatives is thus far incomparable to that observed in Chechnya in the 2000s. While thousands went missing in Chechnya, the number of Dagestanis gone missing is only in the dozens. However, the destruction of insurgents' relatives' homes has recently become a widespread practice in Dagestan, causing outrage among a significant segment of the local population.

In Chechnya, the use or threat of lethal violence against insurgents' relatives has led many predominantly nationalist-minded Chechen insurgents to capitulate or defect. Nevertheless, hundreds of predominantly Salafi-minded individuals chose to remain in the ranks of the insurgent groups. It is arguable whether the smaller-scale use of the practice of forced disappearance of insurgents' relatives and supporters could force Dagestani jihadists — a committed corps of fighters — to capitulate, defect, or disengage. The liquidation of insurgents' relatives' homes or firing them from their positions may even be less relevant for Dagestani jihadists, as many of these jihadists consider martyrdom (*shahada*) to be on the path of jihad — that they consider to be the ultimate goal leading a Muslim to paradise — and a desirable outcome not only for themselves, but also for their families.[225] In Dagestan, the practice of intimidating insurgents through the use of violence against their relatives has thus far not been invoked, but it is unclear whether, and to what extent, it could be effective if deployed against Dagestani jihadists.

The deployment of mop-up operations in Dagestan has the potential to generate a new generation of avengers because, although they have been considerably less violent and more selective in comparison to Chechnya, they have not been without their setbacks. For example, the populations of targeted villages have expressed concern over cases of looting, disrespect toward Islamic symbols, and the liquidation of their homes — all of which violate the local code of honor.[226] Forced disappearances of insurgents' relatives have evoked particular outrage to the point that intimidation has likely led some would-be insurgents, particularly those motivated by personal revenge, to refrain from violent mobilization or pro-insurgent support in order not to endanger their relatives' lives or property. Others, however, driven by the honor-mandated quest for retaliation, seek to avenge the wrongs inflicted on them in spite of these higher costs. This is likely to ensure a constant flow of new recruits into the locally operating *jamaats* and create a vicious cycle of retribution and counter-retribution. In Dagestan, as elsewhere in the North Caucasus, some of the local population is likely to continue providing support to the insurgents, due to both the prevalence of the codes of hospitality and their sympathies for the insurgents.[227]

In Chechnya, it has been the deployment of the *kadyrovtsy* as a numerous,[228] well-equipped, and determined paramilitary force consisting of local men, many of whom are veterans of the previous war, that has stemmed the tide of the armed conflict. The *kadyrovtsy's* knowledge of the local social landscape, the *modi operandi* and *vivendi* of the insurgents — their former fellow fighters — and their identities and social networks have been crucial to their success. The *kadyrovtsy's* large-scale use of violence against the relatives of insurgents and their supporters has also played an immense role in breaking the local insurgency. None of these measures has been put into practice in Dagestan or elsewhere in the North Caucasus to the same extent as in Chechnya, which begs the question as to what makes Chechnya unique in this regard.

One factor is that Dagestani authorities have launched a series of programs to win over insurgents.[229] In addition, the republic's head, Ramazan Abdulatipov, has openly encouraged the establishment of militia or paramilitary units.[230] Modeled after the *kadyrovtsy*, these units would be responsible for fighting insurgent groups in their respective areas; however, there is no evidence thus far of efforts by Dagestani authorities to follow the Chechen example of deploying capitulated or defected insurgents in combat against their former comrades-in-arms. The reasons for this are manifold, and all relate to Dagestan's structural differences from Chechnya. Unlike Chechnya, with its "pacified" public space, which came at the cost of thousands of civilians killed in the two successive wars and in the ruthless counterinsurgency that ensued, Dagestan has experienced no widespread violence of that magnitude.

In the early-2000s, the Russian army deployed largely indiscriminate violence in Chechnya, where they considered virtually any Chechen male of conscription age as a suspect and thus a potential target. While membership in the *kadyrovtsy* units became synonymous with survival for many Chechen youth in the early-2000s, this has not been the case in Dagestan. Dagestan's economy is in considerably better shape than post-war Chechnya's economy was in the early-2000s, when many youth sought to enter the *kadyrovtsy* paramilitaries in order to survive economically. As a result, Dagestani youth do not strive to enter local counterinsurgency militia units.

Dagestan has enjoyed a certain degree of civil liberties that may be considered free by regional standards. In spite of the frequent assassinations of local journalists, relatively free and diverse media still exist in Dagestan. This is in stark contrast to Chechnya, where all media outlets are — without exception — subordinate to Kadyrov. Unlike Chechnya, Dagestan is a republic ruled by oligarchs, serving as champions of their ethnic communities and in turn relying on their support. Another difference between the two republics is that NGOs are active in Dagestan but have been gradually eradicated in Chechnya, with the remnants of human rights organizations and monitors such as Memorial effectively having been pushed out of the republic by the mid-2000s. A hypothetical "Chechenization" of Dagestan, including the installation of an authoritarian regime, the establishment of *kadyrovtsy*-style paramilitaries, and the deployment of large-scale violence against the relatives of local insurgents by those paramilitaries would necessarily run aground Dagestan's intricate ethnic makeup and the associated multitude of power centers. In Dagestan, the emergence of a mono-ethnic autocracy dependent on mono-ethnic paramilitaries and aimed against the republic's multi-ethnic population would entail strong popular dissent among the republic's various ethnic groups, which would fiercely defy such a move. This could result in a series of interethnic clashes that Moscow would barely be able to control. As a largely homogenous entity, the Dagestani insurgency has not witnessed an ideological split between Salafi-jihadists and nationalists—a split that might prompt members of one group to defect to the authorities in order to settle a score with members of the rival group. When combined, these factors explain Moscow's hesitation to install a Chechnya-style regime in Dagestan and its decision to selectively deploy certain counterinsurgency measures adapted to Dagestan's realities.

Infiltration and Decapitation.

The infiltration of jihadist groups has proven to be an effective counterinsurgency practice that has facilitated these groups' gradual breakdown from within. Infiltration has been facilitated by the massive number of recruits joining jihadist groups from the late-2000s until around 2013. Sources from the region nevertheless suggest that, along with the declining number of recruits into jihadist groups, jihadist leadership has become increasingly skeptical of new recruits. Dagestani jihadists, for example, have reintroduced the established mechanism of recruitment. To enter a *jamaat*, a prospective recruit is required to bring along a "recommendation" from at least two jihadists or a reputed Salafi *imam*; his family history is investigated, and he must carry out an initiation killing that is videotaped by fellow fighters.[231] Taken together, these protective steps have reduced the likelihood of insurgent groups being infiltrated by moles, and although infiltration is still possible, this extra time may allow *jamaats* to become operational and conduct violent attacks.

To prevent infiltration, or alleviate the impact of successful infiltrations, Dagestani jihadist groups have increasingly adopted an organizational innovation by reducing membership in *jamaats* from 12 to 15 members to around 7.[232] Currently, only the *amirs* of local *jamaats* are in touch with the *amirs* of neighboring *jamaats*, while ordinary jihadists only interact with their fellow in-group members. As a result, ordinary members increasingly lack personal knowledge of jihadists who are members of other groups. Insurgent groups have also reinforced their autonomy, and since around late-2013, have become increasingly selective and cautious in terms of recruitment, funding, and contacts with outsiders than they previously were.[233]

Overall, decapitation has primarily proven to be an effective counterinsurgency method in the short term. Deprived of experienced leadership, many previously active insurgent groups found themselves incapable of operating. In spite of the paralysis that the jihadist groups experienced in the immediate months following decapitation, however, many have still proven capable of regeneration. As a result, decapitation has been a rather partial success overall, and the incumbents' efforts to infiltrate and decapitate jihadist groups have been confronted by the fragmentation of most jihadist groups.

The North Caucasians' Recruitment to the Syrian Civil War.

The Syrian Civil War has attracted hundreds of North Caucasians since 2011, with these recruits usually joining one of two major jihadist groups: the Islamic State of Iraq and Syria or Levant (ISIS or ISIL, which since 2014 has been renamed into Islamic State) or *Jabhat al-Nusra*. The split between these organizations, accompanied by occasional infighting, has nevertheless disillusioned many North Caucasians, both in the Middle East and in their native region. Disapproval of the Islamic State's brazen brutality has prompted some North Caucasians to turn away from traveling to Syria and to join the local "jihad" instead. Rather than a movement committed to establishing a pious and fair theocracy on the principles of the Prophet Muhammad's early Islamic society, the Islamic State is increasingly viewed as a plot initiated by the United States, Israel, and the West—a view that is consistent with the current attitudes prevailing in Russia.[234] Kadyrov recently encapsulated this increasingly widespread view by pointing to the West as the mastermind of the Islamic State and other similar jihadist organizations with the aim of destroying the Muslim world from within.[235] Against this backdrop, the number of Chechen volunteers to Syria probably reached its peak in 2014,[236] and many young Dagestanis have also lost the desire to travel to Syria as a result of the aforementioned reasons.[237]

Little information is available on the North Caucasian veterans of the Syrian Civil War who have managed to return to their native cities and villages.[238] It is likely that the Russian authorities may either prevent their return to the country, put them in jail, or place them under surveillance in order to track their contacts in the North Caucasus. Those managing to return to the North Caucasus and join the regional insurgency, however, give an important impetus to the insurgency, even if these fighters' numbers are relatively low. The return of these fighters, now-experienced war veterans with connections to established jihadist networks operating elsewhere in the world, back into the North Caucasus may jeopardize Russia's security situation.[239] As noted by Varvara Parkhomenko, an International Crisis Group expert on the North Caucasus, "even if just a small percentage of those fighting there [in Syria] were to return to the North Caucasian insurgency, it could have an immense impact."[240]

Importantly, only a segment of North Caucasians are inspired by Salafi-jihadism, and although the number of individual fighters driven by various motivations is impossible to determine, it is well known that many North Caucasians join the insurgency due to strictly personal motives. These individuals are driven by the need to retaliate — as dictated by the local code of honor — for the wrongdoings inflicted upon them, or in protest of what they consider to be societal sins and injustice. This branch of recruits is significant, because it will continue to remain intact irrespective of the developments in and around Syria.

IV. CONCLUSION

This monograph identified the factors that have contributed to the sharp decline in insurgent violence since 2013. Four major factors were identified: (1) the selective targeting of insurgents and their supporters; (2) the collective punishment of insurgents' relatives; (3) the infiltration and decapitation of insurgent groups; and, (4) the North Caucasians' recruitment into the Syrian Civil War. This monograph has shown that the first three methods were previously deployed in Chechnya, where the incumbent has been relatively successful in critically weakening the local insurgency. These methods have been redeployed in other parts of the North Caucasus, particularly in the hotbed of regional insurgency — Dagestan — and have generally led to a gradual debilitation of the local insurgent groups.

Specifically, the use of selective violence, facilitated by the deployment of elite counterinsurgency units backed by the Russian army, has been conducive to the disruption of ties between the insurgents and their local supporters. Replacing local police as the main counterinsurgency force, these elite forces — comprised predominantly of SOBR and OMON units — have been deployed in special operations, particularly mop-ups and raids. Casualties among the civilian population have largely been avoided, and the deployment of the Russian army, aided by artillery and air force units, against insurgents in Dagestan has helped to isolate the insurgent groups' rural hideouts from urban networks. The Russian Army has also been instrumental in destroying the insurgents' infrastructure, which in turn has left local insurgent groups severely weakened.

The use of collective punishment of insurgents' relatives through extrajudicial executions, forced disappearances, and the liquidation of insurgents' relatives' homes has brought about a rather inconclusive outcome in Dagestan. In this key North Caucasian republic, collective punishment has not taken on massive proportions as was the case in Chechnya in the 2000s. Nevertheless, as a result of newly introduced mop-up operations, dozens of insurgents' relatives have gone missing in Dagestan without a trace — having been abducted under force by federal and local *siloviki*. Dozens of houses belonging to insurgents' families have been deliberately destroyed, with authorities imposing increasingly new and sophisticated forms of collective punishment on the insurgents' relatives. Although these methods may intimidate some of the local population, they are at the same time likely to generate determined avengers who would seek to either join insurgent groups or provide them with support.

Infiltration and decapitation have led to the substantial weakening of impacted insurgent groups. The killing of many experienced and reputed commanders in Chechnya, Dagestan, and elsewhere in the North Caucasus has paralyzed these groups, and instead of carrying out offensive operations, these groups have had to focus on regrouping and selecting new leadership. The growing attraction of the Syrian jihad, coupled with the rise of the increasingly potent jihadist groups operating therein, has compelled hundreds of North Caucasians to travel to the Middle East. Against this backdrop, the Russian authorities took a lax stance to prospective volunteers, thereby enabling its citizens to volunteer in the distant war. This, in turn, has led to the draining of recruits into North Caucasian *jamaats*.

This monograph has illustrated that, while the aforementioned causes have considerably weakened the North Caucasus insurgent groups, they have nevertheless had their limits. Although the deployment of both federal and local elite counterinsurgency forces backed by the Russian military has been instrumental in weakening the local insurgency, these forces have been quite limited numerically. Russia's movement of elite counterinsurgency units from the North Caucasus to Ukraine in 2014, and the subsequent redeployment of these troops to Syria since 2015, has reduced the number of elite troops in the North Caucasus, particularly in Dagestan. The balance of power in this hotbed of regional insurgency therefore appears to be changing already, with insurgent groups increasingly confronting local police units. Should the situation change even further through the growth of local *jamaats* or the deployment of SOBR and OMON units outside of Russia, then local police units would have to replace elite units as the major counterinsurgency force in the region.

Widespread corruption, the salience of nepotism and kinship ties, and the incompetence of local police — with their continued use of indiscriminate violence against the insurgents' alleged supporters and sympathizers — have reduced the effectiveness of the local counterinsurgency. The simultaneous deployment of various branches of security personnel has also been accompanied by inter-institutional animosity between the ethnic-Russian "newcomers" and the local *siloviki*. In contrast to Chechnya, the incumbent has found it difficult to curb the sources of Dagestani *jamaats'* predominantly local funding.

Infiltration of insurgent groups has been an effective counterinsurgency method that was largely facilitated by the large-scale recruitment into jihadist groups in the late-2000s. Since around 2013, confronted with a decrease in the number of prospective recruits, local *jamaats* have become increasingly selective in their recruitment policies. This has made infiltration into their ranks more difficult compared to previous years. Against this backdrop, and coupled with the gradual redeployment of elite counterinsurgency forces beyond the North Caucasus, the previous achievements of the counterinsurgency may be lost. In addition, despite the paralysis that resulted from excessive killings of skilled commanders and veterans of the local insurgency, as well as the loss of much of their operational strength, jihadist groups have still proven to be capable of regrouping under new leadership. It appears that, while infiltration and decapitation have proven to be a successful counterinsurgency measures in the short term, their impact is rather limited in the long term.

In the meantime, the Syrian jihad has lost much of its appeal to many North Caucasians. In recent months, the brazen brutality of the Islamic State prompted many of its sympathizers to turn their back on this jihadist quasi-state. Instead of traveling to the distant Middle East, many frustrated North Caucasians appear to be motivated to stay in their home region and partake in the local "holy war." In the short term, this could lead to the strengthening of the local insurgency, as some of these youth may be likely to join locally operating *jamaats*. While most North Caucasian jihadists are unlikely to make it back to their home region, even a small number of experienced jihadists returning from Syria to the North Caucasus may boost the regional insurgency, as the returning jihadists would bring in new contacts within the international jihadist scene.

This monograph has identified the sources of jihadist groups' viability; however, despite serious blows inflicted upon many of the region's jihadist groups, the insurgents have proven to be a force capable of survival. This could be explained by a combination of factors. First, most insurgents appear to be individual avengers determined to retaliate against the wrongs inflicted upon them by the counterinsurgents' predominantly indiscriminate attacks. Driven by the local custom of blood revenge, avengers will remain an important component of the local insurgency as long as indiscriminate targeting is practiced by local authorities. The lack of serious reforms of security personnel both on the federal and republican levels suggests that the local police force is likely to remain corrupt, incompetent, and incapable of conducting highly selective targeting of insurgents and their supporters. In spite of the high cost stemming from the use of selective violence against insurgents' supporters, some of the local population — driven by the local code of hospitality and their sympathies for the insurgents — has still sought to provide support to the insurgents. Against this endogenous background, external factors, such as developments in other jihadist hotbeds like Syria, will have only a partial impact on the North Caucasian insurgency.

To substantially tear the social fabric of the local insurgency, Moscow could deploy large-scale violence against the relatives of the insurgents, similar to the violence it deployed in Chechnya in the 2000s. It could also place the burden of fighting the insurgents on the shoulders of the local population — particularly former insurgents. Moscow has attempted to establish *kadyrovtsy*-style paramilitary units in Dagestan, which has turned out to be a failed initiative due to the Dagestanis' unwillingness to enter such units.[241] The Russian authorities have nevertheless shown a critical understanding of what these attempts may mean for Dagestani society in comparison to Chechnya's. Due to the multi-ethnic character of Dagestan, its lack of experience in large-scale war, the absence of an authoritarian regime, and the existence of a multitude of ethnic and clan-based power centers, no paramilitary force similar to the *kadyrovtsy* — including those relying on former insurgents — would have been formed in Dagestan. Attempts to establish authoritarian and necessarily mono-ethnic rule would also be counterproductive in Dagestan, where the population would strongly defy such a move to the point of armed resistance, and such attempts would result in interethnic clashes. This is an option that Moscow has thus far sought to avoid in Dagestan; rather than turning Dagestan into a second Chechnya, the Russian authorities have selectively applied a number of counterinsurgency measures in Dagestan that were tested in Chechnya.

The North Caucasus insurgency draws on limited resources, is confined to a relatively small area, and is challenged by a far superior force. While concentrated attacks may substantially weaken it from time to time, it is likely to persist at a latent level and, so long as the factors detailed above linger on, will remain alive for the years to come.

ENDNOTES

1. Luke Harding, "Russia ends anti-terrorism operations in Chechnya," *The Guardian,* April 16, 2009, available from *www.theguardian.com/world/2009/apr/16/russia-chechnya-anti-terrorism,* accessed on October 9, 2015.

2. Michael Schwirtz, "Russia Ends Operations in Chechnya," *The New York Times,* April 16, 2009, available from *www.nytimes.com/2009/04/17/world/europe/17chechnya.html?_r=0,* accessed on October 15, 2015.

3. Emil Souleimanov, "Dagestan: The Emerging Core of the North Caucasus Insurgency," *Central Asia-Caucasus Analyst,* Vol. 12, No. 18, September 29, 2010, available from *www.cacianalyst.org/publications/archive/item/207-caci-analyst-2010-09-29.html,* accessed on August 12, 2015; Emil Souleimanov, "Kabardino-Balkaria Risks Becoming New Insurgency Hotspot," *Central Asia-Caucasus Analyst,* Vol. 13, No. 4, March 2, 2011, available from *www.cacianalyst.org/publications/archive/item/216-caci-analyst-2011-03-02.html,* accessed on October 13, 2015; The Jamestown Foundation, "Insurgency-Related Violence Reported in Dagestan, Kabardino-Balkaria and Ingushetia," *North Caucasus Weekly,* Vol. 12, Iss. 22, November 18, 2011.

4. Mairbek Vatchagaev, "The Karachay Jamaat: Alive and Operational," *Eurasia Daily Monitor,* Vol. 9, Iss. 118, June 21, 2012; Emil Souleimanov, "North Ossetia: Jihadization in the Making?" *Central Asia-Caucasus Analyst,* Vol. 13, No. 11, June 8, 2011, available from *www.cacianalyst.org/publications/archive/item/223-caci-analyst-2011-06-08.html,* accessed on October 13, 2015.

5. Emil Souleimanov, "North Caucasus Insurgency Makes Inroads to Tatarstan, Bashkortostan," *Central Asia-Caucasus Analyst,* Vol. 15, No. 11, May 29, 2013, available from *www.cacianalyst.org/publications/archive/item/12752-caci-analyst-may-29-2013.html,* accessed on October 13, 2015.

6. Quoted in Aslan Doukaev, "Is Khloponin The Right Man For The North Caucasus?" *Radio Free Europe/Radio Liberty,* Commentary, October 9, 2010, available from *www.rferl.org/content/Is_Khloponin_The_Right_Man_For_The_North_Caucasus/2185521.html,* accessed on October 13, 2015.

7. *Ibid.*

8. At the time, this unprecedented display of the jihadists' resolve and good organization was considered to be a humiliation of Russia's intelligence and secret services. Emil Souleimanov, "Volgograd Bombings Demonstrate the Inability of Russia's Security Services," *Central Asia-Caucasus Analyst*, Vol. 16, No. 1, January 8, 2014, available from *www.cacianalyst.org/publications/analytical-articles/item/12890-volgograd-bombings-demonstrate-the-inability-of-russias-security-services.html*, accessed on August 12, 2015.

9. Emil Souleimanov, "The Republic of Dagestan: the epicenter of Islamist insurgency in Russia's North Caucasus," *IPRIS*, Vol. 4, December 2011.

10. Data from the Kavkazskiy uzel news site summarized in Huseyn Aliyev, "Conflict-related Violence Decreases in the North Caucasus as Fighters go to Syria," *Central Asia-Caucasus Analyst*, Vol. 17, No. 6, April 1, 2015, available from *www.cacianalyst.org/publications/analytical-articles/item/13171-conflict-related-violence-decreases-in-the-north-caucasus-as-fighters-go-to-syria.html*, accessed on August 12, 2015; Liz Fuller, "Why Is The Death Toll Tumbling In The North Caucasus?" *Radio Free Europe/Radio Liberty*, Caucasus Report blog, February 10, 2015, available from *www.rferl.org/a/insurgency-north-caucasus-terrorism-isis/26840778.html,* accessed on October 13, 2015.

11. "Zhertvami Vooruzhennogo Konflikta na Severnom Kavkaze v Pervom Kvartale 2015 Goda Stali 51 Chelovek" ("In the First Quarter of 2015, 51 Fell Victim to the Armed Conflict in the North Caucasus"), Kavkazskiy uzel, April 24, 2015, available from *www.kavkaz-uzel.ru/articles/261215/*, accessed on September 1, 2015.

12. Based on Kavkazskiy uzel's statistics. According to official sources, insurgents formed the most casualties.

13. For a recent analysis of the situation of the local insurgency, see, for instance, Huseyn Aliyev, "Revival of Islamist Insurgency in the North Caucasus?" *Central Asia-Caucasus Analyst*, October 14, 2016, available from *cacianalyst.org/publications/analytical-articles/item/13403-revival-of-islamist-insurgency-in-the-north-caucasus?.html*, accessed on October 22, 2016.

14. Andrew E. Kramer and Neil MacFarquhar, "Fierce Attack by Islamist Militants in Chechen Capital Kills at Least 20," *The New York Times*, December 4, 2014, available from *www.nytimes.com/2014/12/05/world/europe/grozny-chechnya-attack.html*, accessed on October 13, 2015; Emil Souleimanov, "Attacks in Grozny Unlikely to Revive the Chechen Insurgency," *Central Asia-Caucasus Analyst*, Vol. 16, No. 23, December 10, 2014, available from *www.cacianalyst.org/publications/analytical-articles/item/13110-attacks-in-grozny-unlikely-to-revive-the-chechen-insurgency.html*, accessed on October 13, 2015.

15. Mairbek Vatchagaev, "Was the December 4 Rebel Attack in Grozny Aimed at Tarnishing the Images of Putin and Kadyrov?" *Eurasia Daily Monitor*, Vol. 11, Iss. 221, December 11, 2014.

16. Author's estimates based on discussions with experts.

17. Aliyev, "Revival of Islamist insurgency in the North Caucasus?"

18. Mairbek Vatchagaev, "Increased Insurgent Activity Reported in Chechnya," *Eurasia Daily Monitor*, Vol. 12, Iss. 46, March 12, 2015.

19. *Ibid.*

20. "Troe Voennosluzhashchikh Podorvalis' na Mine v Chechne" ("Three Troops Trapped by a Mine in Chechnya"), Kavkazskiy uzel, August 9, 2015, available from *www.kavkaz-uzel.ru/articles/266907/*, accessed on August 19, 2015.

21. "Ivanov: na Severnom Kavkaze Vse Yeshche Slozhnaya Kriminogennaya Obstanovka" ("In the North Caucasus, a Difficult Criminogenic Situation Persists"), *Gazeta*, February 26, 2015.

22. Languages belonging to the Nakho-Dagestani (Chechen; Ingush; and various Dagestani languages including Avar, Dargin, Lak, Lezgin), Adyghe or Circassian (Cherkes, Kabardin, Adyg, Abaza), Iranian (Ossetian, Tat), Turkic (Karachay-Balkar, Kumyk, Noghai), and Slavic (Russia, Ukrainian) language families dominate the ethnolinguistic landscape of the North Caucasus.

23. For an analysis of Islam as a discursive phenomenon in the Caucasus and Chechnya, see Sofie Bedford and Emil Souleimanov, "Under construction and highly contested: Islam in the post-Soviet Caucasus," *Third World Quarterly*, Vol. 37, Iss. 9, 2016, pp. 1559-1580.

24. Historically, the present-day Stavropol and Kranodar provinces also used to be part of the North Caucasus. As these provinces are now inhabited predominantly by a Slavic and partially by a non-Slavic — for example, Armenians and Meskhetian Turks — population of non-indigenous origin, the Stavropol and Krasnodar provinces are treated separately from the "ethnic" rest of the North Caucasus.

25. Lesley Blanch, *The Sabres of Paradise: Conquest and Vengeance in the Caucasus,* London: Tauris Parke Paperbacks, 2004.

26. In contrast, since the 1860s, hundreds of thousands of Adyghe (Circassian) peoples were exiled from their homeland to the Ottoman Empire, with their land given predominantly to Cossacks and Russian colonists.

27. For a discussion of the number of casualties, see, for instance, John B. Dunlop, "How many soldiers and civilians died during the Russo-Chechen war of 1994–1996?" *Central Asian Survey*, Vol. 19, No. 3–4, 2000, p. 338.

28. John B. Dunlop, *Russia Confronts Chechnya: Roots of a Separatist Conflict,* New York: Cambridge University Press, 1998.

29. Emil Souleimanov, "Chechnya, Wahhabism and the Invasion of Dagestan," *Middle East Review of International Affairs (MERIA)*, Vol. 9, No. 4, December 2005, pp. 68-100.

30. Domitilla Sagramoso, "The Radicalisation of Islamic Salafi *Jamaats* in the North Caucasus: Moving Closer to the Global *Jihadist* Movement?" *Europe-Asia Studies*, Vol. 64, Iss. 3, 2012, pp. 561-595; see also Julie Wilhelmsen, "Between a Rock and a Hard Place: The Islamisation of the Chechen Separatist Movement," *Europe-Asia Studies*, Vol. 57, Iss. 1, January 2005, pp. 35-59. For an analysis of the recruitment strategies of Chechnya's Salafi-jihadists in the interwar period, see Emil A. Souleimanov, "Jihad or Security?

Understanding the Jihadization of Chechen Insurgency through Recruitment into Jihadist Units," *Journal of Balkan and Near Eastern Studies,* Vol. 17, Iss. 1, 2015, pp. 86-105.

31. Jean-François Ratelle and Emil Aslan Souleimanov, "Retaliation in Rebellion: The Missing Link to Explaining Insurgent Violence in Dagestan," *Terrorism and Political Violence,* forthcoming in 2017, published online March 17, 2015, available from *www.tandfonline.com/doi/full/10.1080/09546553.2015.1005076.* See also Emil Souleimanov, *An Endless War: The Russian-Chechen Conflict in Perspective,* Frankfurt, Germany: Peter Lang, 2007.

32. For more information on the causes and contexts of the establishment of the Caucasus Emirate (CE), see, for instance, Emil Souleimanov, "The Caucasus Emirate: Genealogy of an Islamist Insurgency," *Middle East Policy,* Vol. 18, Iss. 4, Winter 2011, pp. 155-168; Stephen Blank and Younkyoo Kim, "The North Caucasus: Russia's Other War," *The Journal of Slavic Military Studies,* Vol. 29, Iss. 2, 2016, pp. 185-202; Stephen Blank, "Russia's Caucasus Wars: The Wrecks of Empire and the Wars of Decolonization," *American Foreign Policy Interests,* Vol. 34, Iss. 4, 2012, pp. 182-193.

33. Interestingly, this organization found its way onto the U.S. list of terrorist groups as late as 2011.

34. Souleimanov, "The Caucasus Emirate."

35. Clan or patrimonial family as a social institution has largely faded away in the Northwestern Caucasus, while family ties have remained strong even in Karachayevo-Cherkesiya and Kabardino-Balkaria.

36. In addition to these practices, nepotism drawing on the sense of shared clan or family identity has remained strong in the North Caucasus.

37. Note that females are exempt from the practice of blood revenge. In Dagestan, as elsewhere in the North Caucasus beyond Chechnya and Ingushetia, retaliation is almost exclusively aimed at the actual culprit himself. It rarely, if at all, targets the actual culprit's relatives.

38. *Malaya Sovetskaya Entsiklopedia* (*Little Soviet Encyclopaedia*), Vol. 1, Moscow, Russia: Sovetskaya Entsiklopedia, 1928. p. 960 c.

39. Author's numerous discussions with North Caucasians.

40. From the interwar period (1920-1941) onward, this custom has been influenced by the criminal code of honor, known as *vorovskoy zakon* (thieves' code) in Russian, and associated primarily with the tradition of the criminals-in-law, *vor z zakone*.

41. Souleimanov, *An Endless War*, pp. 205-209.

42. For a detailed overview of the socioeconomic and political situation in the North Caucasus, see Elena Pokalova, *Chechnya's Terrorist Network: The Evolution of Terrorism in Russia's North Caucasus*, Santa Barbara, CA: Praeger, 2015, pp. 144-147.

43. See "Uroven Bezrabotitsi v Chechne Dostig 80-ti Protsentov" ("Unemployment in Chechnya Reached 80 Percent"), Kavkazskiy uzel, April 5, 2005, available from *www.kavkaz-uzel.ru/articles/72602/*, accessed on July 8, 2014.

44. "Russian unemployment ranges from 1.2% in St. Petersburg to 31.1% in Ingushetia — Rosstat," *Interfax*, October 20, 2014, available from *www.interfax.com/newsinf.asp?id=545081*, accessed on October 9, 2015.

45. William Ascher, author, Natalia Mirovitskaya, ed., *Development Strategies, Identities, and Conflict in Asia*, New York: Palgrave Macmillan, 2013, p. 159.

46. Alexander Auzan and Sergey M. Bobylev, eds. (Russian), Ben W. Hooson, ed. (English), *Modernization and Human Development*, National Human Development Report for the Russian Federation 2011, Moscow, Russia: United Nations Development Programme, 2011.

47. Natalia Zubarevich, *Sotsial`no-ekonomicheskoe razvitie respublik Severnogo Kavkaza: kolichestvennye i ekspertnye otsenki in Portrety Regionov (The Socio-Economic Development of the North Caucasus Republics: Quantitative and Expert Assessments, in: The Portraits of [Russian] Regions)*, Moscow: Nezavisimyi Institut Sotsial`noi Politiki, 2010.

48. *Ibid.*

49. Tom Parfitt, "Trouble in the North Caucasus," *The Guardian,* June 22, 2009 available from *www.theguardian.com/ commentisfree/2009/jun/22/ingushetia-president-assassination-caucasus,* accessed on October 9, 2015.

50. Dagestan's former President, Mukhu Aliyev, quoted in Tony Wood, *Chechnya: The Case for Independence,* London, UK: Verso, 2007, p. 140.

51. "Opros: Zhiteli Dagestana Nazvali Tri Glavnye Prichiny Vspleska Nasiliya v Respublike" ("Survey: Dagestan's Inhabitants Name Three Main Reasons for Violence"), *Caucasus Times,* May 10, 2013.

52. Robert Bruce Ware and Enver Kisriev, *Dagestan: Russian Hegemony and Islamic Resistance in the North Caucasus,* Armonk, NY: M. E. Sharpe, 2010, pp. 62-73.

53. Author's numerous discussions with Dagestanis.

54. The Russians comprise around 22 percent of Kabardino-Balkaria's population.

55. Gordon M. Hahn, *Russia's Islamic Threat,* New Haven, CT: Yale University Press, 2007; Sergey Markedonov, *Radical Islam in the North Caucasus: Evolving Threats, Challenges, and Prospects,* CSIS Reports, Washington, DC: Center for Strategic & International Studies, 2010; Robert W. Schaefer, *The Insurgency in Chechnya and the North Caucasus: From Gazavat to Jihad,* Santa Barbara, CA: Praeger Security International, 2011; Lorenzo Vidino, "How Chechnya Became a Breeding Ground for Terror," *Middle East Quarterly,* Vol. XII, No. 3, Summer 2005, pp. 57-66; Paul J. Murphy, *The Wolves of Islam: Russia and the Faces of Chechen Terror,* Dulles, VA: Brassey's, 2004; Yossef Bodansky, *Chechen Jihad: Al Qaeda's Training Ground and the Next Wave of Terror,* New York: Harper Collins, 2007.

56. Hahn, *Russia's Islamic Threat,* p. 14.

57. For a comprehensive analysis of these allegations, see Brian Glyn Williams, "Shattering the Al-Qaeda-Chechen Myth: Part I," *North Caucasus Weekly,* Vol. 4, Iss. 35, October 2, 2003; Brian

Glyn Williams, "Shattering the Al-Qaeda-Chechen Myth (Part II): Exploring the Links Between the Chechen Resistance and Afghanistan," *North Caucasus Weekly*, Vol. 4, No. 40, November 6, 2003.

58. Andrew McGregor, "Ghost Soldiers: Osama bin Laden's Chechen Legion," *Shout!* June-July 2002.

59. *Ibid.*

60. See, for instance, Sagramoso, "The Radicalisation of Islamic Salafi *Jamaats* in the North Caucasus."

61. Bodansky. For a critical analysis of this approach, see, for instance, Emil Souleimanov and Ondrej Ditrych, "The Internationalisation of the Russian-Chechen Conflict: Myths and Reality," *Europe-Asia Studies*, Vol. 60, Iss. 7, 2008, pp. 1199-1222. For a nuanced analysis of the phenomenon of Arab foreign fighters in the Chechen wars, see Cerwyn Moore and Paul Tumelty, "Foreign Fighters and the Case of Chechnya: A Critical Assessment," *Studies in Conflict & Terrorism*, Vol. 31, Iss. 5, 2008, pp. 412-433; Cerwyn Moore, "Foreign Bodies: Transnational Activism, the Insurgency in the North Caucasus and 'Beyond'," *Terrorism and Political Violence*, Vol 27, Iss. 3, 2015, pp. 395-415.

62. For a nuanced analysis of this process, see, for instance, James Hughes, *Chechnya: From Nationalism to Jihad,* Philadelphia, PA: University of Pennsylvania Press, 2007.

63. In Russia, authorities have traditionally rejected their share of responsibility for the violence in the region or its indigenous roots, presenting it instead as an imported affair.

64. Jean-François Ratelle, "A critical assessment of the scholarship on violent conflicts in the North Caucasus during the post-Soviet period," *Caucasus Survey,* Vol. 3, Iss. 1, 2015, p. 7.

65. Matthew Evangelista, *The Chechen Wars: Will Russia Go the Way of the Soviet Union?* Washington, DC: Brookings Institution Press, 2002; Wilhelmsen; Ekaterina Sokirianskaya, "State and Violence in Chechnya (1997–1999)," in Anne Le Huérou, Aude Merlin, Amandine Regamey, and Elisabeth Sieca-Kozlowski,

eds., *Chechnya at War and Beyond*, Abingdon: Routledge, 2014, pp. 93-117.

66. Souleimanov, "Chechnya, Wahhabism and the Invasion of Dagestan."

67. Georgi M. Derluguian, *Bourdieu's Secret Admirer in the Caucasus: A World-System Biography*, Chicago, IL: University of Chicago Press, 2005; Souleimanov, *An Endless War*; Sokirianskaya.

68. Emil Souleimanov and Huseyn Aliyev, *The Individual Disengagement of Avengers, Nationalists, and Jihadists: Why Ex-Militants Choose to Abandon Violence in the North Caucasus*, Basingstoke: Palgrave Macmillan, 2014.

69. Anne Speckhard and Khapta Ahkmedova, "The Making of a Martyr: Chechen Suicide Terrorism," *Studies in Conflict & Terrorism*, Vol. 29, Iss. 5, 2006, pp. 429-492.

70. Jean-François Ratelle, "The North Caucasus insurgency: understanding the Chechen rebels in the context of the Caucasus Emirate," in Anne Le Huérou, Aude Merlin, Amandine Regamey, Elisabeth Sieca-Kozlowski, eds., *Chechnya at War and Beyond*, Abingdon: Routledge, 2014, p. 188.

71. See information presented further in this monograph.

72. In this regard, the North Caucasian experience of jihadist radicalization is similar to the same process in other parts of the world, including Muslim diaspora communities in the West. See, for instance, Rachel Briggs and Jonathan Birdwell, "Radicalisation Among Muslims in the UK," *Microcon Policy Working Paper 7*, Brighton: Microcon, 2009; Mehdi Hasan, "The Muslim faith does not turn men to terror: The two suspects in the Woolwich killing were violating the doctrine of their own holy book," *The Telegraph*, May 23, 2013.

73. Souleimanov, "Jihad or Security?" Souleimanov and Aliyev, *The Individual Disengagement of Avengers, Nationalists, and Jihadists*. Yet this is a common experience that scholars have observed in the case of, for instance, non-religious nationalist terrorist, and insurgent groups as well.

74. Ratelle, "A Critical Assessment of the Scholarship."

75. Souleimanov, "Jihad or Security?"

76. "North Caucasus: The Challenges of Integration (II), Islam, the Insurgency and Counter-Insurgency," *Crisis Group Europe Report N°221*, Brussels, Belgium: Headquarters, International Crisis Group, October 19, 2012, p. 15.

77. For a discussion on the religious aspects of the North Caucasus insurgency, see, for instance, Ratelle, "A Critical Assessment of the Scholarship," p. 9.

78. For an overview of this debate, see, for instance, Doug Saunders, "What Turns Some Western Muslims Into Terrorists? The Causes of Extremism," Doug Saunders blog, entry posted April 25, 2013, available from *www.dougsaunders.net/2013/04/muslim-immigrants-terrorists-jihad-terrorism/*, accessed on October 13, 2015.

79. See, for instance, Stephen J. Blank, *Russia's Homegrown Insurgency: Jihad in the North Caucasus,* Carlisle, PA: Strategic Studies Institute, U.S. Army War College, 2012.

80. Vicken Cheterian, *War and Peace in the Caucasus: Ethnic Conflict and the New Geopolitics*, New York: Columbia University Press, 2008. See Derluguian; Domitilla Sagramoso, "Violence and conflict in the Russian North Caucasus," *International Affairs*, Vol. 83, Iss. 4, July 27, 2007, pp. 681-705; Jean-François Ratelle, *Radical Islam and the Chechen War Spillover: A Political Ethnographic Reassessment of the Upsurge of Violence in the North Caucasus Since 2009*, Doctoral Thesis, Ottawa, Canada: University of Ottawa, 2013, available from *www.ruor.uottawa.ca/handle/10393/23791?locale=fr*, accessed on August 14, 2015.

81. Derluguian; Cheterian.

82. Valery Tishkov, *Ethnicity, Nationalism and Conflict in and after the Soviet Union: The Mind Aflame*, London, UK: SAGE Publications, 1997; Valery Tishkov, *Chechnya: Life in a War-Torn Society*, Berkeley, CA: University of California Press, 2004; Brian Glyn Williams, "From 'Secessionist Rebels' to 'Al Qaeda Shock Brigades': Assessing Russia's Efforts to Extend the Post-Septem-

ber 11th War on Terror to Chechnya," *Comparative Studies of South Asia, Africa and the Middle East,* Vol. 24, No. 1, 2004, pp. 197-209; Aurélie Campana, "The Effects of War on the Chechen National Identity Construction," *National Identities,* Vol. 8, Iss. 2, 2006, pp. 129-148.

83. Christoph Zürcher, *The Post-Soviet Wars: Rebellion, Ethnic Conflict, and Nationhood in the Caucasus,* New York: New York University Press, 2007.

84. To be precise, some authors have studied greed-related factors of violent mobilization, particularly in Chechnya. See Tishkov, *Chechnya: Life in a War-Torn Society,* p. 104; Mark Galeotti, "'Brotherhoods' and 'Associates': Chechen Networks of Crime and Resistance," *Low Intensity Conflict & Law Enforcement,* Vol. 11, Iss. 2-3, 2002, pp. 340-352. While greed postulates that individuals mobilize to acquire material benefits, in Chechnya, however, a reverse order applied. Chechen insurgents or warlords became interested in, for example, securing their share of Chechnya's oil fields in the interwar period, not during, or prior to the First Chechen War. The present author shows the gradual transformation of some Dagestani jihadist groups into organized crime groups interested in collaborating with the authorities for the sake of the personal enrichment of the leadership of these jihadist groups, see Emil Souleimanov, "Dschihadisten in Dagestan: Clans, Kompromisse und krumme Geschäfte" ("Jihadists in Dagestan: Clans, Compromises and Crooked Business"), *Osteuropa: Zeitschrift für Gegenwartsfragen des Ostens,* Vol. 65, No. 4, 2015, pp. 115-129. This phenomenon, however, is rather confined to the borders of Dagestan, with only several known jihadist groups engaging in such activities. Otherwise, the lethality rate among North Caucasian insurgents is too high, and the prospects of acquiring material benefits nearly absent, for greed to be a motivating factor for individuals to join insurgent groups.

85. Emil Aslan Souleimanov and Huseyn Aliyev, "Evaluating the efficacy of indigenous forces in counterinsurgency: Lessons from Chechnya and Dagestan," *Small Wars & Insurgencies,* Vol. 27, Iss. 3, 2016, pp. 392-416; Mairbek Vatchagaev, "Police Violence in Dagestan Continues as Republic Drifts Toward Collapse From Within," *Eurasia Daily Monitor,* Vol. 11, Iss. 91, May 15, 2014; Nabi Abdullaev, "A Murderous Cycle of Revenge in Dagestan," *The Moscow Times,* March 15, 2005.

86. Emil Souleimanov, "The Upsurge of Islamist Violence in the North Caucasus: Exploring the Case Studies of Dagestan and Kabardino-Balkaria," *Connections: The Quarterly Journal*, Vol. 10, No. 3, Summer 2011, pp. 117-126; Alissa De Carbonnel, "Insight: Brutality, anger fuel jihad in Russia's Caucasus," Reuters, August 31, 2012, available from *www.reuters.com/article/2012/08/31/us-russia-dagestan-idUSBRE87U09R20120831*, accessed on October 13, 2015.

87. "Human Rights Watch: Voyna bez voyny. Narusheniya prav cheloveka v khode borby rossiyskikh vlastey s vooruzhennym podpolyem v Dagestane" ("A War without a War: Human Rights Violations During the Russian Authorities' Fights Against the Armed Resistance in Dagestan"), Kavkazskiy uzel, June 26, 2015, available from *www.kavkaz-uzel.ru/articles/264623/*, accessed on August 19, 2015.

88. Interview conducted by the author with Sapiyat Magomedova, Prague, March 2014.

89. Ratelle and Souleimanov; Jean-François Ratelle, "Making sense of violence in civil war: challenging academic narratives through political ethnography," *Critical Studies on Security*, Vol. 1, Iss. 2, 2013, pp. 159-173; Souleimanov and Aliyev, *The Individual Disengagement of Avengers, Nationalists, and Jihadists*.

90. Emil Aslan Souleimanov and Huseyn Aliyev, "Blood Revenge and Violent Mobilization: Evidence from the Chechen Wars," *International Security*, Vol. 40, Iss. 2, Fall 2015, pp. 158-180; Ratelle and Souleimanov.

91. Ratelle and Souleimanov; Cerwyn Moore, "Suicide Bombing: Chechnya, the North Caucasus and Martyrdom," *Europe-Asia Studies*, Vol. 64, Iss. 9, 2012, pp. 1780-1807.

92. Souleimanov and Aliyev, *The Individual Disengagement of Avengers, Nationalists, and Jihadists*; Ratelle and Souleimanov.

93. Elections of the heads of autonomous republics were abolished in the mid-2000s on the pretext of improving Russia's security after the terrorist attack in the North Ossetian town of Beslan in September 2004.

94. "North Caucasus: The Challenges of Integration (IV), Economic and Social Imperatives," *Crisis Group Europe Report N°237*, Brussels, Belgium: Headquarters, International Crisis Group, July 7, 2015; Valery Dzutsati, "Russia Fears Possible Tectonic Shifts in the North Caucasus," *Eurasia Daily Monitor*, Vol. 12, Iss. 73, April 20, 2015, note: the *Eurasia Daily Monitor* uses "Dzutsati" as the spelling of this author's last name; an alternate spelling of "Dzutsev" is used by other publications, see endnote 142; Andrew C. Kuchins, Matthew Malarkey and Sergei Markedonov, *The North Caucasus: Russia's Volatile Frontier*, CSIS Russia and Eurasia Program Report, Washington, DC: Center for Strategic & International Studies (CSIS), March 2011, pp. 14-16.

95. Roland Dannreuther and Luke March, "Chechnya: Has Moscow Won?" *Survival: Global Politics and Strategy*, Vol. 50, Iss. 4, 2008, p. 108.

96. Emil Souleimanov and Maya Ehrmann, "The Rise of Militant Salafism in Azerbaijan and Its Regional Implications," *Middle East Policy*, Vol. XX, No. 3, Fall 2013; Alexey Malashenko, "Islamic Challenges to Russia, From the Caucasus to the Volga and the Urals," Carnegie Moscow Center, May 13, 2015, available from *carnegie.ru/2015/05/13/islamic-challenges-to-russia-from-caucasus-to-volga-and-urals/i9l4*, accessed on October 14, 2015.

97. Valery Dzutsati, "Support for Salafists Among Dagestani Youth Reaches Record Level," *Eurasia Daily Monitor*, Vol. 8, Iss. 227, December 14, 2011.

98. Ratelle and Souleimanov.

99. Author's personal observations.

100. Jean-Charles Brisard, "Terrorism Financing: Roots and trends of Saudi terrorism financing," Report prepared for the President of the Security Council United Nations, *JCB Consulting*, December 19, 2002, p. 9, available from *www.investigativeproject. org/documents/testimony/22.pdf*, accessed on October 14, 2015; Ariel Cohen, "A Threat to the West: The Rise of Islamist Insurgency in the Northern Caucasus and Russia's Inadequate Reponse," *Backgrounder No. 2643*, Washington, DC: The Heritage Foundation, March 26, 2012, available from *www.heritage.org/research/*

reports/2012/03/a-threat-to-the-west-the-rise-of-islamist-insurgency-in-the-northern-caucasus#_ftnref55, accessed on October 14, 2015.

101. Schaefer, p. 172.

102. Charlotte Hille, *State Building and Conflict Resolution in the Caucasus,* Leiden, Netherlands: Brill, 2010, p. 301.

103. Mark Mackinnon, "Will use any tactic, Chechen warlord warns," *The Globe and Mail,* November 2, 2004, available from *www.theglobeandmail.com/news/world/will-use-any-tactic-chechen-warlord-warns/article1006369/,* accessed on October 15, 2015.

104. "The role of Al-Qaeda in the North Caucasus," Agentu-ra.ru, September 13, 2010, available from *www.agentura.ru/english/terrorism/alqaedanc/,* accessed on October 15, 2015.

105. Associated Press (Moscow), "Putin says US helped North Caucasus separatists against Russia in the 2000s," *The Guardian,* April 26, 2015, available from *www.theguardian.com/world/2015/apr/26/putin-us-helped-north-caucasus-separatists-russia-bush,* accessed on October 15, 2015.

106. For an overview of his claims, see Reuters, "Think Tank Says Al-Qaeda Funding Caucasus Rebels," *Radio Free Europe/Radio Liberty,* News, September 30, 2011, available from *www.rferl.org/a/think_tank_says_alqaeda_funding_caucasus_rebels/24344410.html,* accessed on October 15, 2015.

107. "Z Česka šly peníze na podporu teroristům z al-Kajdy" ("Money Transferred from the Czech Republic to Support al-Qaeda Terrorists"), Týden, May 5, 2011, available from *www.tyden.cz/rubriky/domaci/z-ceska-sly-penize-na-podporu-teroristum-z-al-kajdy_200911.html,* accessed on October 15, 2015.

108. Emil A. Souleimanov and Huseyn Aliyev, "Asymmetry of Values, Indigenous Forces, and Incumbent Success in Counter-insurgency: Evidence from Chechnya," *Journal of Strategic Studies,* Vol. 38, No. 5, 2015, pp. 678-703.

109. Author's discussions with experts on the local insurgency.

110. Souleimanov, "Dschihadisten in Dagestan: Clans, Kompromisse und krumme Geschäfte" ("Jihadists in Dagestan: Clans, Compromises and Crooked Business"). See also Emil Aslan Souleimanov, "Making Jihad or Making Money? Understanding the Transformation of Dagestan's *Jamaats* into Organised Crime Groups," *Journal of Strategic Studies*, forthcoming in 2017, published online December 28, 2015, available from *dx.doi.org/10.1080 /01402390.2015.1121871*.

111. Dzutsati, "Support for Salafists Among Dagestani Youth Reaches Record Level."

112. Author's discussions with Russian and Dagestani experts and journalists.

113. Emil Souleimanov and Huseyn Aliyev, *How Socio-Cultural Codes Shaped Violent Mobilization and Pro-Insurgent Support in the Chechen Wars*, Basingstoke: Palgrave Macmillan, 2017.

114. For a comprehensive analysis of this transformation, see, for instance, Hughes.

115. Three additional *vilayats* have existed since its establishment in 2007: the *vilayats* of Iriston of North Ossetia, of Cherkessia (including Cherkessia and the Adyghean autonomous republic, formally part of the Krasnodar province), and of the Noghay steppe (including the Noghai-dominated parts of Dagestan and the Stavropol province). In 2009, the North Ossetian *vilayat* was formally abolished by Dokka Umarov and incorporated into the Ingush *vilayat*. The remaining two *vilayats* have been nearly absent from the self-representation of the Caucasus Emirate-affiliated jihadists, due to the lack of insurgent groups in those areas.

116. Emil Souleimanov, "Caucasus Emirate Faces Further Decline after the Death of Its Leader," *Central Asia-Caucasus Analyst*, April 29, 2015, available from *www.cacianalyst.org/publications/ analytical-articles/item/13188-caucasus-emirate-faces-further-decline- after-the-death-of-its-leader.html*, accessed on October 15, 2015.

117. The most important jihadist groups, represented by their leaders in the *Majlis ash-Shura* (consultative council), take part in the election of the *amir* of the Caucasus Emirate. In addition

to this consultative body, the Caucasus Emirate has its supreme judge *(qadi)* who utilizes sharia law to arbitrate disputes. In recent years, facing increasingly fierce counterinsurgency, these two institutions have become rather formal as insurgent leaders from across the North Caucasus can scarcely meet to make collective decisions. Given the fragmented character of the Caucasus Emirate's organization, the *qadi's* decisions are hardly enforceable by a supreme authority outside the radius of his insurgent group.

118. Gordon M. Hahn, *The Caucasus Emirate Mujahedin: Global Jihadism in Russia's North Caucasus and Beyond,* Jefferson, NC: McFarland & Company, Inc., 2014, p. 256.

119. Islam Tekushev, "Triumph of the Caucasus Emirate: The Caucasus Emirate as a Special Ethno-Fundamentalist Model," *Islam, Islamism and Politics in Eurasia Report (IIPER),* No. 52, February 17, 2012, pp. 9-20.

120. Cerwyn Moore, "A Review of Martyrdom Operations and the Insurgency in the North Caucasus: 2008 to the Present," *Eurasia Daily Monitor,* Vol. 8, No. 34, February 17, 2011, available from *https://jamestown.org/program/a-review-of-martyrdom-operations -and-the-insurgency-in-the-north-caucasus-2008-to-the-present-2/,* accessed on October 28, 2016.

121. Ian R. Kenyon, "The Chemical Weapons Convention and OPCW: The Challenges of the 21st Century," *The CBW Conventions Bulletin,* Iss. 56, June 2002, p. 15.

122. Emil Souleimanov, "Dagestan's Jihadists and Haram Targeting," *Central Asia-Caucasus Analyst,* Vol. 17, No. 3, February 18, 2015, available from *www.cacianalyst.org/publications/analytical- articles/item/13140-dagestan's-jihadists-and-haram-targeting.html,* accessed on October 15, 2015.

123. Schaefer, pp. 233-270.

124. For a comprehensive analysis of the geography of the North Caucasus insurgency, see John O'Loughlin, Edward C. Holland and Frank D. W. Witmer, "The Changing Geography of Violence in Russia's North Caucasus, 1999-2011: Regional Trends and Local Dynamics in Dagestan, Ingushetia, and Kabardino-

Balkaria," *Eurasian Geography and Economics,* Vol. 52, Iss. 5, 2011, pp. 1-35.

125. See, for instance, Souleimanov, *An Endless War,* pp. 168-169.

126. Quoted in Mark Kramer, "The Perils of Counterinsurgency: Russia's War in Chechnya," *International Security,* Vol. 29, Iss. 3, 2004, p. 9.

127. Until his assassination in May 2004, Akhmad Kadyrov was head of the Kadyrov family. Kadyrov was part of the Chechen separatist elites and was appointed *mufti* — or head — of Chechnya's Muslims in 1995, during the peak of the First Russo-Chechen War. Kadyrov apparently took a direct part in the war on the Chechens' side. During the interwar period, he supported Aslan Maskhadov in his confrontation with the country's increasingly vocal and ambitious jihadist elites. Following the onset of hostilities in 1999, Kadyrov — known for his anti-Salafi position — criticized Maskhadov for his inability to cope with the jihadist challenge. Facing the arrival of the Russian army in Gudermes, the second-largest Chechen city controlled by Kadyrov loyalists, Kadyrov decided to hand the city to the Russians without firing a single shot in order to avoid bloodshed. Following Akhmad Kadyrov's assassination, his son Ramzan succeeded him as Chechnya's (in)formal head.

128. Emil Souleimanov, "An Ethnography of Counterinsurgency: *Kadyrovtsy* and Russia's Policy of Chechenization," *Post-Soviet Affairs,* Vol. 31, No. 2, 2015, pp. 91-114; Emil Aslan Souleimanov, Huseyn Aliyev, Jean-François Ratelle, "Defected and loyal? A case study of counter-defection mechanisms inside Chechen paramilitaries," forthcoming in *Terrorism and Political Violence* in 2017, published online July 11, 2016, available from *dx.doi.org/10.1080/09546553.2016.1194270.*

129. Souleimanov, "An Ethnography of Counterinsurgency."

130. *Ibid;* Emil Souleimanov, "Russian Chechnya Policy: 'Chechenization' Turning Into 'Kadyrovization'?" *Central Asia-Caucasus Analyst,* May 31, 2006, available from *https://www.caci-*

analyst.org/publications/analytical-articles/item/10873-analytical-arti-cles-caci-analyst-2006-5-31-art-10873.html, accessed on October 28, 2016.

131. On some occasions, and particularly during the early stages of the armed conflict, the *kadyrovtsy* carried out attacks against their former enemies or relatives (those unrelated to the insurgency), as well as indiscriminate attacks on some villagers.

132. Emil Aslan Souleimanov and David S. Siroky, "Random or Retributive?: Indiscriminate Violence in the Chechen Wars," *World Politics,* Vol. 68, No. 4, 2016, pp. 677-712. See also Emil Souleimanov and David Siroky, "The Logic of Killing Kin in the Irregular War: Evidence from Chechnya," *Comparative Politics,* forthcoming in 2017.

133. "Russia/Chechnya: The 'Dirty War' in Chechnya: Forced Disappearances, Torture, and Summary Executions," *Human Rights Watch,* Vol. 13, No. 1 (D), March 1, 2011, available from *https://www.hrw.org/report/2001/03/01/dirty-war-chechnya-forced-disappearances-torture-and-summary*, accessed on October 14, 2015.

134. Nick Paton Walsh, "Chechen government admits civilians buried in mass graves," *The Guardian,* June 15, 2005, available from *www.theguardian.com/world/2005/jun/16/chechnya.russia,* accessed on March 21, 2014.

135. Importantly, due to fears of penalization and impunity, many Chechen families chose not to report their hijacked relatives. "Chechnya, 2004 god. Pokhishcheniya i ischeznoveniya ludey" ("Chechnya, 2004. Abductions and Disappearances"), Memorial, February 8, 2005, available from *polit.ru/article/2005/02/08/memo/,* accessed on January 15, 2013.

136. Souleimanov and Siroky, "Random or Retributive?"

137. Author's numerous discussions with Chechen émigrés in Europe and Russia, 2007-2013.

138. *Ibid.*

139. "Worse than a War: 'Disappearances' in Chechnya—a Crime Against Humanity," *Human Rights Watch Briefing Paper*, March 2005, available from *hrw.org/backgrounder/eca/chechnya0305/*, accessed on October 15, 2015.

140. Shura Burtin, "Kadyrov ne spravlaetsa" ("Kadyrov is Failing"), *Expert,* July 14, 2009, available from *expert.ru/2009/07/14/sobutiya_kavkaz/*, accessed on October 6, 2015.

141. "Chechnya: 'Siloviki' Ispolzuyut Rodstvennikov Boevikov v Kachestve Zhivogo Shchita" ("Chechnya: Law Enforcement Uses the Insurgents' Relatives as a Shield"), Memorial, September 9, 2010, available from *www.memo.ru/2010/09/09/0909101. htm*, accessed on February 12, 2014.

142. For an analysis of the nature of Ramzan Kadyrov's regime in Chechnya, his personal relationship with Vladimir Putin, and the sources of his power, see Emil Aslan Souleimanov and Grazvydas Jasutis, "The dynamics of Kadyrov's regime: between autonomy and dependence," *Caucasus Survey*, Vol. 4, Iss. 2, 2016, pp. 115-128. For an analysis of the phenomenon of Chechnya's (and North Caucasus') pro-Moscow elites through the prism of indirect rule theory, see, for instance, David S. Siroky, Valery Dzutsev, and Michael Hechter, "The differential demand for indirect rule: evidence from the North Caucasus," *Post-Soviet Affairs,* Vol. 29, Iss. 3, 2013, pp. 268-286.

143. Souleimanov and Siroky, "Random or Retributive?" Tanya Lokshina, "Dispatches: Burning Down the House in Chechnya," *Human Rights Watch,* December 10, 2014, available from *https://www.hrw.org/news/2014/12/10/dispatches-burning-down-house-chechnya*, accessed on October 15, 2015.

144. Dmitry Volchek, "'Absolute Schizophrenia' Reigns In Kadyrov's Chechnya, Says Filmmaker," *Radio Free Europe/Radio Liberty*, North Caucasus March 15, 2015, available from *www.rferl.org/content/russia-chechnya-kadyrov-documentary-loizeau/26902320.html*, accessed on October 15, 2015.

145. Souleimanov and Siroky, "Random or Retributive?"

146. *Ibid.*

147. Interview with Ekaterina Sokirianskaya, January 2014.

148. These wrongs have often included severe torture, killing, or humiliation—particularly rape—of insurgents or their relatives at the hands of the *kadyrovtsy*.

149. Souleimanov, "Attacks in Grozny Unlikely to Revive the Chechen Insurgency."

150. Interview with Abdulla Istamulov, June 2014.

151. "Five killed in suicidal bombing in Chechen capital," BBC News, October 5, 2014, available from *www.bbc.com/news/world-europe-29498909*, accessed on October 15, 2015.

152. Liz Fuller, "Was The Insurgent Attack On Grozny A Trial Run?" *Radio Free Europe/Radio Liberty*, Caucasus Report blog, December 6, 2014, available from *www.rferl.org/a/grozny-attack-chechnya/26728961.html*, accessed on October 15, 2015.

153. Souleimanov and Aliyev, "Asymmetry of Values, Indigenous Forces, and Incumbent Success in Counterinsurgency."

154. "Report Tells How FSB Targeted Basayev," *The Moscow Times*, March 27, 2007, available from *www.pressreader.com/russia/the-moscow-times/20070327/281569466277140*, accessed on October 27, 2016.

155. Putin decorated 26 people at the time, including two men. *Ibid*.

156. Kenyon, p. 47.

157. Valeriy Lebedev, "Chechenskiy Khirurg Khasan Bayev" ("Chechen Surgeon Khasan Bayes"), *Vestnik*, Vol. 11, No. 244, May 23, 2000, available from *www.vestnik.com/issues/2000/0523/koi/lebedev.htm*, accessed on October 20, 2015.

158. "Russian Security Had Mole in Chechens Who Attacked Theater," *Agence France Presse*, April 28, 2003, available from *https://www.aei.org/publication/russian-security-had-mole-in-chechens-who-attacked-theater/*, accessed on October 15, 2015.

159. "Российские спецслужбы травят чеченских боевиков ядом" ("Russian Secret Services Poison Chechen Fighters"), Newsland, July 2015, *newsland.com/news/detail/id/539538/*, accessed October 2015.

160. *Ibid.* Interestingly, Chechen authorities have claimed that they annihilated those slain insurgents in combat.

161. *Ibid.*

162. These units have been intensely deployed in Dagestan and other areas of the North Caucasus since early-2013.

163. See, for instance, Mumin Shakirov, "V Dagestane Sozda-yutsa Novie Podrazdeleniya Spetsnaza" ("New Units of Spetsnaz are Being Formed in Dagestan"), Newsland, September 27, 2010, available from *newsland.com/news/detail/id/563403/*, accessed on August 14, 2015.

164. Author's consultations with Russian and North Cauca-sian security experts, 2014-2015.

165. These counterterrorism departments have in fact large-ly drawn on the local police force. Lacking proper training and equipment, they have numbered only several hundred service-men. Units of the republican directorates of the Russian security service *Federalnaya Sluzhba Bezopasnosti* (FSB), known by the ac-ronym (UFSB), which are by far a more competent force, have also been deployed. Due to the proliferation of insurgent groups, particularly in Dagestan, these numerically weak forces neverthe-less soon ceased to adequately confront the jihadists.

166. Alissa De Carbonnel, "Insight: Russia fears return of fighters waging jihad in Syria," Reuters, November 14, 2013, available from *www.reuters.com/article/2013/11/14/us-russia-caucasus-syria-insight-idUSBRE9AD05Q20131114*, accessed on October 15, 2015.

167. Emil Souleimanov, "What Does Amirov's Arrest Imply for Dagestan?" *Central Asia-Caucasus Analyst*, Vol. 15, No. 13, June 26, 2013.

168. Souleimanov, "Dschihadisten in Dagestan: Clans, Kompromisse und krumme Geschäfte" ("Jihadists in Dagestan: Clans, Compromises and Crooked Business").

169. Souleimanov and Aliyev, *How Socio-Cultural Codes Shape Violent Mobilization and Pro-Insurgent Support in the Chechen Wars*.

170. Amounts have ranged from $10,000 to $100,000 U.S. dollars, depending on function. Author's numerous discussions with Dagestanis, 2007-2013.

171. Souleimanov, "What Does Amirov's Arrest Imply for Dagestan?"

172. Souleimanov and Aliyev, "Evaluating the Efficacy of Indigenous Forces in Counterinsurgency."

173. *Ibid.*

174. Mairbek Vatchagaev, "Russian Counter-Terrorism Operations Return to Ingushetia," *Eurasia Daily Monitor*, Vol. 12, Iss. 123, July 1, 2015, available from *https://jamestown.org/program/russian-counter-terrorism-operations-return-to-ingushetia-2/*, accessed on October 28, 2016; Valery Dzutsati, "Six Suspected Rebels Killed in Kabardino-Balkaria," *Eurasia Daily Monitor*, Vol. 12, Iss. 140, July 27, 2015; "Counter-terrorist operation regime declared in Nalchik, in North Caucasus," *Russian News Agency*, June 30, 2015, available from *tass.ru/en/russia/804827*, accessed on October 10, 2015.

175. "Vse voprosy dolzhny reshatsya v ramkakh zakona, a ne po adatam" ("All Problems Should Be Solved According to Law, not Adat"), *Kommersant*, January 11, 2013, available from *www.kommersant.ru/doc-y/2102663*, accessed on August 10, 2015.

176. Valery Dzutsati, "Redeployment of Russian Forces to Ukraine Leads to Drop in Violence in North Caucasus," *Eurasia Daily Monitor*, Vol. 12, Iss. 8, January 14, 2015.

177. Fuller, "Why Is The Death Toll Tumbling In The North Caucasus?"

178. Emil Souleimanov, "Mopping up Gimry: 'Zachist-kas' Reach Dagestan," *Central Asia-Caucasus Analyst*, Vol. 15, No. 8, April 17, 2013, available from *https://www.cacianalyst.org/publications/archive/item/12711-caci-analyst-april-17-2013.html*, accessed on August 14, 2015.

179. "'Invisible War' Russia's Abusive Response to the Dagestan Insurgency," *Human Rights Watch Report*, June 18, 2015, available from *https://www.hrw.org/report/2015/06/18/invisible-war/russias-abusive-response-dagestan-insurgency*, accessed on October 15, 2015.

180. The incumbent has reapplied experience from counter-insurgency operations in Chechnya, where similar tactics were applied.

181. Author's numerous discussions with experts and ordinary Dagestanis.

182. According to a report by Kavkazskiy uzel cited by *Radio Free Europe/Radio Liberty*, around 20,000 troops were deployed in Dagestan. Liz Fuller, "Confusion Surrounds Reported Troop Deployment to Daghestan," *Radio Free Europe/Radio Liberty*, Caucasus Report blog, March 20, 2012, available from *www.rferl.org/a/confusion_surrounds_reported_troop_deployment_to_daghestan/24522096.html*, accessed on October 15, 2015.

183. Emil Souleimanov, "Russia Redeploys Army to Dagestan," *Central Asia-Caucasus Analyst*, Vol. 14, No. 23, November 14, 2012, available from *https://www.cacianalyst.org/publications/archive/item/236-caci-analyst-2012-11-14.html*, accessed on August 14, 2015; Souleimanov, "Dagestan's Jihadists and Haram Targeting."

184. A group calling itself the Black Hawks was formed in Kabardino-Balkaria in 2011; it called for a Chechnya-style retributive liquidation of insurgents' relatives as a legitimate means of fighting the local insurgency. See, for instance, Liz Fuller, "Who Are Kabardino-Balkaria's 'Black Hawks'?" *Radio Free Europe/Radio Liberty*, Caucasus Report blog, February 24, 2011, available from *www.rferl.org/a/who_are_kabardino-balkaria_back_hawks/2319966.html*, accessed on October 15, 2015.

185. Mairbek Vatchagaev, "Kabardino-Balkaria's 'Black Hawks:' Grassroots Vigilantes or FSB Surrogates?" *Eurasia Daily Monitor*, Vol. 8, Iss. 49, March 11, 2011, available from *https://jamestown.org/program/kabardino-balkarias-black-hawks-grassroots-vigilantes-or-fsb-surrogates/*, accessed on October 15, 2015.

186. "Members of 'execution list' leave Dagestani village of Khadjalmakhi, local reports," Caucasian Knot, April 10, 2013, available from *eng.kavkaz-uzel.ru/articles/23670/*, accessed on October 15, 2015 (Caucasian Knot is the English branch of the previously cited Russian news site, Kavkazskiy uzel).

187. "Duma Passes New Anti-Terror Bill," *The Moscow Times*, October 27, 2013, available from *www.themoscowtimes.com/news/article/duma-passes-new-anti-terror-bill/488531.html*, accessed on October 15, 2015.

188. "'Invisible War' Russia's Abusive Response to the Dagestan Insurgency," *Human Rights Watch Report*, pp. 29-39.

189. *Ibid*, p. 32.

190. Interview conducted by the author with Ekaterina Sokirianskaya, head of the Russian office of the International Crisis Group, September 10, 2015.

191. According to most experts, these disappearances are to be attributed to the authorities' efforts to punish either the insurgents' relatives or, most commonly, to punish their (alleged) supporters by destroying the insurgents' support networks.

192. Author's personal estimates, based on the analysis of open sources (Kavkazskiy uzel, Human Rights Watch, Memorial) and consultations with experts and human rights activists in Russia and the North Caucasus.

193. Irina Gordienko, "Stvoly Rubyat Pod Koren. Posle Unichtozheniya Boevikov Dagestanskogo "Lesa" Siloviki Vzyalis Za Ikh Rodstvennikov" ("Trees are Being Cut at the Root. Having liquidated the Dagestani Fighters, Law Enforcement Have Embarked on Their Relatives"), *Novaya Gazeta*, September 7, 2015, available from *www.novayagazeta.ru/politics/69826.html*, accessed on October 15, 2015.

194. Mairbek Vatchagaev, "The Evolution of Salafism in the North Caucasus," *Eurasia Daily Monitor*, Vol. 9, Iss. 157, August 16, 2012.

195. Souleimanov, "Caucasus Emirate Faces Further Decline after the Death of Its Leader."

196. Mairbek Vatchagaev, "Why Do Jamaat Leaders Die so Often in North Caucasus Special Operations?" *Eurasia Daily Monitor*, Vol. 11, Iss. 212, November 26, 2014.

197. Liz Fuller, "Gakayev Deaths Leave One Campfire Less In Chechen Mountains," *Radio Free Europe/Radio Liberty*, Caucasus Report blog, January 30, 2013, available from *www.rferl.org/a/chechen-insurgency-commanders-killed-gakayev/24887859.html*, accessed on October 15, 2015.

198. Liz Fuller, "Suspected 'Mole' Who Allegedly Betrayed Chechen Insurgency Group to Face Trial," *Radio Free Europe/Radio Liberty*, Caucasus Report blog, July 25, 2013, available from *www.rferl.org/a/caucasus-chechen-insurgency-mole-temishev-trial/25057148.html*, accessed on October 15, 2015.

199. Emil Souleimanov, "Gakayev Brothers Killed in Chechnya," *Central Asia-Caucasus Analyst*, Vol. 15, No. 3, February 6, 2013, available from *https://www.cacianalyst.org/publications/archive/item/12642-caci-analyst-february-6-2013.html*, accessed on August 14, 2015.

200. Souleimanov, "Caucasus Emirate Faces Further Decline after the Death of Its Leader."

201. Liz Fuller, "Six North Caucasus Insurgency Commanders Transfer Allegiance To Islamic State," *Radio Free Europe/Radio Liberty*, Caucasus Report blog, January 2, 2015, available from *www.rferl.org/a/islamic-state-north-caucasus-insurgency-commanders-allegiance/26773615.html*, accessed on October 15, 2015; See also Mark Youngman, "Between Caucasus and caliphate: the splintering of the North Caucasus insurgency," *Caucasus Survey*, Vol. 4, Iss. 3, 2016, pp. 194-217; Emil Souleimanov, "Dagestan's Insurgents Split over Loyalties to Caucasus Emirate and IS," *Central Asia-Caucasus Analyst*, April 15, 2015, Vol. 17, No. 7, available

from *www.cacianalyst.org/publications/analytical-articles/item/13177-dagestan's-insurgents-split-over-loyalties-to-caucasus-emirate-and-is.html,* accessed on October 15, 2015; Emil Souleimanov, "Umarov's (Non)Resignation: Is the North Caucasus Insurgency Becoming Divided?" *Central Asia-Caucasus Analyst,* August 19, 2010, Vol. 12, No. 15, available from *https://www.cacianalyst.org/publications/analytical-articles/item/12111-analytical-articles-caci-analyst-2010-8-19-art-12111.html,* accessed on October 16, 2015.

202. De Carbonnel, "Insight: Russia Fears Return of Fighters Waging Jihad in Syria."

203. For an overview of the North Caucasians volunteers' motivations to take part in the Syrian Civil War, see Jean-François Ratelle, "North Caucasian foreign fighters in Syria and Iraq: assessing the threat of returnees to the Russian Federation," *Caucasus Survey,* Vol. 4, Iss. 3, 2016, pp. 218-238; Emil A. Souleimanov, "Globalizing Jihad? North Caucasians in the Syrian Civil War," *Middle East Policy,* Vol. 21, Iss. 3, Fall 2014, pp. 154-162. For the causes of Russia's declared withdrawal from Syria, see, for instance, Emil Aslan Souleimanov, "Mission Accomplished? Russia's Withdrawal from Syria," *Middle East Policy,* Vol. 23, Iss. 2, Summer 2016, pp. 108-118.

204. "FSB RF: V Ryadakh Boevikov v Irake Voyuyut Pochti Dve Tysiachi Rossiyan" ("In the Fighters' Ranks, Almost Two Thousand Russians Are Combating"), *Rossiyskaya gazeta,* February 20, 2015.

205. A different situation has prevailed in Chechnya, where, due to heavy control over the local population, Chechnya's authorities have been able to trace the identities of missing youth, with the relatives of dozens of Chechen youth who have reportedly traveled to Syria subjected to penalization. It comes as no surprise that most Chechen volunteers in Syria appear to come either from northern Georgia's Chechen-populated Pankisi Gorge or from Chechen diaspora communities scattered across Europe.

206. Emil Aslan Souleimanov and Katarina Petrtylova, "Russia's Policy toward the Islamic State," *Middle East Policy,* Vol. 22, Iss. 3, Fall 2015, pp. 66-78; Interview conducted by the author with Akhmet Yarlykapov, a Russian-Dagestani anthropologist with

the Russian Academy of Sciences' Institute of Ethnology and Anthropology, September 2015; Souleimanov, "Globalizing Jihad? North Caucasians in the Syrian Civil War."

207. Aliyev, "Conflict-related Violence Decreases in the North Caucasus as Fighters go to Syria."

208. Souleimanov and Petrtylova, "Russia's Policy toward the Islamic State."

209. *Ibid.*

210. Discussions by the author with officers of the Dagestani branch of the Russian Ministry of Interior, May 2015.

211. *Ibid.*

212. On the contrary, search-and-destroy operations in the mountainous terrain are usually conducted by SOBR units or, in the case of Chechnya, by the *kadyrovtsy*.

213. Interestingly, unlike the Special Purpose Mobility Units, *Otryad Mobilny Osobogo Naznacheniya* (OMON) units, the Special Rapid Response Units, *Spetsial'nye Otryady Bystrogo Reagirovaniya* (SOBR) consist exclusively of officers.

214. Author's consultations with Russian security experts and journalists.

215. Gabriela Baczynska, Tom Perry, Laila Bassam and Phil Stewart, "Exclusive: Russian troops join combat in Syria—sources," Reuters, September 10, 2015, available from *www.reuters.com/article/2015/09/10/us-mideast-crisis-syria-exclusive-idUSKCN0R91H720150910*, accessed on October 15, 2015.

216. "Ukraine crisis: 'Russian special forces' captured," BBC News, May 17, 2015, available from *www.bbc.com/news/world-europe-32776198*, accessed on October 15, 2015; Dzutsati, "Redeployment of Russian Forces to Ukraine Leads to Drop in Violence in North Caucasus."

217. Valery Dzutsati, "War With Ukraine Pulls Best Russian Military Units From North Caucasus," *Eurasia Daily Monitor*, Vol. 11, Iss. 156, September 8, 2014.

218. Quoted in *ibid*.

219. Discussions by the author with Russian and Dagestani experts and journalists from May to September 2015.

220. "'Invisible War': Russia's Abusive Response to the Dagestan Insurgency," *Human Rights Watch Report*, pp. 28-41.

221. Author's consultations with Russian and Dagestani journalists and experts, 2014-2015.

222. Souleimanov, "Russia Redeploys Army to Dagestan."

223. Author's consultations with Russian and Dagestani journalists and experts, 2014-2015.

224. For example, all Chechen state employees are required to pay around 10 percent of their monthly income to the Akhmad Kadyrov Foundation, which is in fact Ramzan Kadyrov's personal fund. Employees from the private sector pay around a third of their earnings to this fund, while business owners are required to pay as much as the half of their income. See, for instance, "Khodorkovsky's NGO reveals incriminating documentary about Ramzan Kadyrov," Meduza, May 25, 2015, available from *https://meduza.io/en/news/2015/05/25/khodorkovsky-s-ngo-reveals-incriminating-documentary-about-ramzan-kadyrov*, accessed on October 15, 2015. Kadyrov has unlimited personal control over this fund and is not accountable to anyone for how he uses these funds. In addition, Kadyrov has routinely embezzled the money that Chechnya receives from the federal budget.

225. Souleimanov, Aliyev, *The Individual Disengagement of Avengers, Nationalists, and Jihadists*.

226. Souleimanov, "Mopping up Gimry: 'Zachistkas' Reach Dagestan."

227. Author's consultations with Russian and Dagestani journalists and experts, 2014-2015.

228. Since the early-2010s, the *kadyrovtsy* have numbered approximately 7,000 fighters.

229. Diana Alieva, "Was Dagestan's Amnesty a Fiction?" *Institute for War and Peace Reporting*, CRS Report No. 386, April 6, 2007, available from *https://iwpr.net/global-voices/was-dagestans-amnesty-fiction*, accessed on October 15, 2015; Huseyn Aliyev, "Dagestan's Commission for Rehabilitation of Rebel Fighters: A Failed Experiment?" *Central Asia-Caucasus Analyst*, Vol. 15, No. 4, February 20, 2013, available from *www.cacianalyst.org/publications/archive/item/12658-caci-analyst-february-20-2013.html*, accessed on October 15, 2015.

230. "Рамазан Абдулатипов: «Необходимо усилитьпроф илактическую работу»" ("Ramazan Abdulatipov: 'We Need to Strengthen Prevention Efforts'"), *RIA Dagestan*, January 18, 2014, available from *www.riadagestan.ru/news/president/ramazan_abdulatipov_neobkhodimo_usilit_profilakticheskuyu_rabotu/*, accessed on April 14, 2015.

231. The victim of this initiation killing is usually a member of the local authorities or, most commonly, a police officer. Insurgents assume that a mole would be unwilling to kill one of their own. Discussion by the author with an officer of the Dagestani Ministry of Interior, May 2015.

232. Discussion by the author with an officer of the Dagestani Ministry of Interior, May 2015.

233. Discussion by the author with an officer of the Dagestani Ministry of Interior, May 2014.

234. Souleimanov and Petrtylova, "Russia's Policy toward the Islamic State."

235. See, for instance, Mairbek Vatchagaev, "Is Russia Training Chechen Commandos to Help Syrian Government Forces?" *Eurasia Daily Monitor*, Vol. 12, Iss. 168, September 18, 2015.

236. Mairbek Vatchagaev, "Has the Number of Chechens Fighting in Syria Reached Its Peak?" *Eurasia Daily Monitor,* Vol. 11, Iss. 14, January 23, 2014.

237. Discussions by the author with ordinary Dagestanis as well as Russian and Dagestani journalists in 2015. In addition, Turkey's deteriorating relations with the Islamic State and the greater difficulty for North Caucasian volunteers to cross the Turkish-Syrian border may further complicate their way to local jihadist groups.

238. Such information is available only on the native North Caucasians residing outside the region, where the risk of penalization of jihadist veterans is low. This includes, for example, Chechen volunteers from northern Georgia's Chechen-dominated Pankisi Gorge. For a first-hand analysis of the situation in the Pankisi area, see Grazvydas Jasutis, "Explaining the Chechen schism in Georgia's Pankisi valley," *Caucasus Survey,* Vol. 3, Iss. 2, 2015, pp. 124-135.

239. See, for instance, Dmitry Shlapentokh, "Russia Fears Jihadists Returning Home," *Central Asia-Caucasus Analyst,* Vol. 16, No. 9, May 7, 2014, available from *www.cacianalyst.org/ publications/analytical-articles/item/12970-russia-fear-jihadists-returning-home.html,* accessed on October 15, 2015.

240. Karina Gadjiyeva and Aida Magomedova, "Eksperty Schitayut Situatsiyu na Severnom Kavkaze Opasnoy i Prognoziruyut Eskalatsiyu Konflikta" ("Experts Consider the Situation in the North Caucasus Dangerous and Predict an Escalation of the Conflict"), Kavkazskiy uzel, January 7, 2015, available from *www.kavkaz-uzel.ru/articles/255197/#.VK0WYXSbdM8.twitter,* accessed on August 15, 2015.

241. Unlike the *kadyrovtsy,* the Dagestani militia—the republic's proposed counterinsurgency force—is not intended to contain former insurgents.

U.S. ARMY WAR COLLEGE

Major General William E. Rapp
Commandant

*****

STRATEGIC STUDIES INSTITUTE
and
U.S. ARMY WAR COLLEGE PRESS

Director
Professor Douglas C. Lovelace, Jr.

Director of Research
Dr. Steven K. Metz

Author
Dr. Emil Aslan Souleimanov

Editor for Production
Dr. James G. Pierce

Publications Assistant
Ms. Denise J. Kersting

*****

Composition
Mrs. Jennifer E. Nevil